GAETANO'S TRUNK

Alfred M. Zappalà
Gaetano's Trunk; Completing the Circle
ISBN 1881901-82-3

Cover design by Catie Rae Zappalà.

Printed in Canada.

For information and for orders, write to:

Legas

P.O. Box 149
Mineola, New York
11501, USA

3 Wood Aster Bay
Ottawa, Ontario
K2R 1D3 Canada

legaspublishing.com

ALFRED M. ZAPPALÀ, ESQ.

Gaetano's Trunk

COMPLETING THE CIRCLE

LEGAS

To Jennifer, Matt, Catie, Rose, John, Noey and little Matthew
My children and grandchildren...and my inspiration in life.

ACKNOWLEDGEMENT

I would like to thank the people of Sicily who throughout their history suffered the yoke of oppression as conqueror after conqueror enslaved them, persecuted them and took anything and everything that Sicily had to offer from them.

To this day, they persevere. Their sacrifices are acknowledged.

We now embrace their identity as ours and struggle to make the future a better place for those who live there today, for those who live in other parts of the world but whose hearts remain in Sicily, and for those who have not yet discovered her beauty.

On a personal level, I'd like to thank those readers of my first book "The Reverse Immigrant" who read it, passed it on to others, and then sent me notes of joy and gratitude. This book is a continuation of my love story with my Island.

I also want to thank my gifted and talented daughter Catie Rae Zappalà who photographed and designed the front and back covers of this book and also want to thank my eldest daughter Jennifer Zappalà McComiskie who took the photo for the back cover.

I want to thank my cousin Madeline Ponti-Bartig who did a pre-edit for me prior to shipping it off to the editor Gaetano Cipolla of Legas, my publisher. Special thanks to ChristineLeone.com for photo edits.

I also want to thank all my friends in Sicily and here in America who inspired me to jot down these thoughts for you.

My goal with this book is that maybe by the time you finish reading it, you too will be inspired to learn more about Bedda Sicilia.

I hope so.

Alfred M. Zappalà

Whenever possible I used the Sicilian word for what I was describing and the Italian word only as a last resort.

Contact Information:
Website: www.alfredzappala.com
Email: alfredzappala@yahoo.com

Contents

BURGATEDDA

By Nino Martoglio

pensi forsi a la to genti,
chi custritta ad emigrari
ti lassò sula sulidda
senza mancu salutari?-

Ma nun c'era altirnativa
siddu partiri o ristari,
c'era sulu lu bisognu,
tanti vucchi di sfamari!

Burgatedda risulenti,
senti a mia, nun ti allarmari,
sti gintuzzi a lu partiri,
sannu gia' ch'hannu a turnari,

e sarà gran festa quannu
rivirrannu li to mura,
tali e quali a primavera
rinnineddi migratura!-

Little Village

By Nino Martoglio
Translated by Gaetano Cipolla

Perhaps you're thinking of your people
who were forced to emigrate
and just left you all alone
without even a good bye?

No alternative existed
to the leaving or remaining,
there was only the great need,
with so many mouths to feed.

Little village full of smiles,
listen carefully, don't fret,
your good people as they left,
knew already they'd return,

and that day will be a feast
they will see your walls again,
like migrating little swallows
that return when springtime comes.

An Introduction (of Sorts)

Come, sit down…I want to talk with you.

Let's have an *espresso* or an *Amaro Averna*. I want to tell you about my Sicily.

I am not an "expert" on Sicily, although I happen to know quite a bit about it. The experts can teach you the nuances of her history. I just want to sit here and talk with you.

I want to talk to you in this book in the same manner as I did in my last book *The Reverse Immigrant,* that is, in a very informal way.

I want you to feel that just you are I are talking…in a café somewhere…preferably in Sicily…and you are listening to me tell you a story.

I am quite good at telling stories. You'll see.

After all, I am a lawyer, and no one tells more stories than a lawyer now, do they?

I also am a law professor, and I much prefer this style of writing when I talk about my Sicily as opposed to that stilted scholarly stuff that puts me to sleep.

Nothing about *Bedda Sicilia* puts me to sleep. I eat breath, live, sleep, dream and love my Island.

No, it is not a perfect place…don't get me wrong.

As I write these words, Italy herself is tottering on the brink of economic ruination. The downturn in the economy has really hurt her.

Sicily, the poor step child of Italy, is in far worse shape.

Yes, there is a mafia (I do not capitalize the "m" in mafia…frankly it isn't worth the effort) in Sicily.

Let's get that out of the way immediately. This book isn't about the mafia. They won't bother you unless you are a criminal. Pay no mind.

Rather, this book is about Sicily's people and places that I have seen and experienced.

The Good Lord gave me a talent…of being able to paint a picture with words… and perhaps one or two of my stories will make you laugh, or make you cry, or give you something to think about, or motivate you to learn about my *Isola Bella.*

That's my real objective...to whet your appetite to learn about your cultural background.

I made the decision two years ago to uproot myself and move to Sicily. I want to live the rest of my life there (except when I come home to see my children and grandchildren, which will be often).

My children love Sicily too, and they *WANT* me to move there.

Thus, my fate is set: During the worse economic crisis since the Great Depression, I am moving there.

In a sense, I am going against the current. I am fighting the head wind.

I do not care. My people need an advocate there. I am sure that even at my old age I can be of some use to someone, can't I?

What you will read and experience in my book are things that happened to an old friend of yours...me...as I open my heart to you, and let you peer inside.

Thus, on second thought, forget that I am a lawyer. To you, we are friends...best friends.

Any mistakes, inaccuracies, typos, misspellings, misstatements are purely mine and I take full responsibility. Take my errors in stride; like you would a stain on a fine piece of leather. This is my story, and we are, after all, friends.

When the Good Lord calls me someday, I will have the following put on a gravestone in Sicily. It will be in French.

French? Yes. Only in French can I express what I want on my marker: "Je ne regrette rien"... I regret nothing.

Thus, sit back, have biscotti, and let me tell you about my Sicily.

Thank you for spending time with me....I appreciate it...a lot.

Alfred M. Zappalà

Gaetano's Trunk

For many years, I have lugged an old steamer trunk with me no matter where I have lived.

There is nothing very special about this trunk. It is green and large, has a couple brass lock-type things, and is a tad beat up. My mom had it in her house.

When she passed on, it became mine. She wanted me to have it.

Over the years, I stored it in the basement and it became a catch-all for useless things that one accumulates over time. In retrospect, I dishonored this trunk by neglecting it so, but I will make amends.

Now, it is my most treasured possession.

Lately, I have been thinking about that trunk and the reasons why I have dragged this thing around with me all these years. The reasons why are beginning to now dawn on me.

Let me tell you the story:

Gaetano's Trunk as it awaits its final trip home.

Back in the early twentieth century, when millions of Italians and Sicilians (along with millions of other Europeans) flocked to America's shores, they packed what little possessions they had into these trunks and took them with them as they made their way across the Atlantic in cramped ocean liners.

They traveled in steerage class…in the bowels of these boats…in cramped and dangerous conditions…and ultimately made it to the shores of America.

At the docks of New York, Boston, Philadelphia, New Orleans and other seaport cities in America, after clearing customs and being subjected to health check-ups, name changes, humiliation, and even isolation, they all ended up on that dock.

With that trunk.

Their life's possessions contained in a box. Things that you and I would probably discard ultimately, but to them the contents of that trunk represented a link to their homeland.

With that trunk, upon re-opening it, they began their life anew… strangers in a strange land.

Those possessions, however meager, were the foundation of a new life in a foreign and exciting new land. I am sure that they packed sentimental things when they packed their trunk; perhaps a photo or two of treasured relatives; maybe some clothing and a remembrance of their ancestral village.

They packed something in each trunk to keep the memory of where they came from burning bright in their minds and their souls.

Now, with that trunk, they were in America.

My trunk is a handsome fellow. It is pretty large. It is dark green in color, about thirty six inches high and wide, forty-eight inches long.

It has wood slats to give it strength and sturdy handles to lift it. It has two big brass locks to secure its contents.

Taken together, this trunk was tasked with carrying the possessions of someone across the world.

My grandfather.

Gaetano Torrisi. Years later, he would father my mom, Antoinette.

I lugged that trunk from house to house all these years as a testament to him. That trunk had a mission…actually two missions…and for a century has yet to complete its last mission.

It has stood silently and proudly in my basement(s) awaiting its final mission.

Today, I assigned to it a final mission. Today it will begin the task of completing the circle of life.

Completing what my grandfather started one hundred and eight years ago. After all, this is Gaetano's Trunk, isn't it?

Today, I decided that this trunk will return to its place of origin.

It is going back to Sicily with me. It will contain my personal possessions when I make my move there in a very few months.

It will complete what was started by him over a century ago.

That trunk will be proud as it performs its final task. It will hold in it the hope and dreams of a heroic man who came to a new land in search of a better life, and now it will hold in it the hopes and dreams of his descendant who will return to his native soil.

A steamer trunk.

Gathering dust and waiting patiently all these years to complete the circle of life.

That trunk is now my most treasured possession. The contents inside are extra, I think.

Who was Gaetano? You know him.

Don't we all have a Gaetano?

I think yes.

I think that I will tell you a bit about him as my story unfolds.

For you see, his story is really your story.

Micho

His nickname didn't fit his name.

"Micho" (pronounced: MEE-JOO) was the nickname for a person named Domenic, and his name was Gaetano.

What he did back in Sicily was take his father's nickname, which WAS Domenic and who had died when he was five years old.

Micho lived with his mother Maria in Valguarnera and soon, both were forced to move to the big city of Catania.

Maria met a man named Pietro and had three more children. Thus Micho had two step brothers and a step sister.

He sprouted like a strong weed; stable and strong. However, as the son of another man, he realized that it would be a matter of time before he would have to move on to create his own existence.

That's the way it was in those days.

He became a street kid, and by age ten or eleven was roaming the streets of Catania trying to find himself. He eventually drifted to Trecastagni, a small village town up on the mountain heading to Etna where he was taken in by the Gangi family.

Today we would call that sort of thing an "equitable adoption". That is, while the Gangi family looked after him as a son, the paperwork was never done.

In those days, not much paperwork was done. Most people couldn't read or write.

Periodically, he would visit his mother Maria in Catania, now immersed in raising her new family.

Micho realized that Maria's life was with her new husband and children and he knew that his path in life would be decided only by him.

The Gangi family has a daughter named Concetta and soon they were married. He was trained in two professions: that of a blacksmith and that of a wine maker.

By the age of eighteen, he had a son, Thomas.

Things being the way they were back then, news began to reach Sicily of the "gold" that lined the streets of America.

My grandfather Gaetano Torrisi and my grandmother Concetta Gangi Torrisi in the prime of their lives. His steely determination and grit became a family hallmark.

Sicily was in terrible shape; no work, no money, constant outbreaks of influenza, so cousins of the Gangis where Micho lived decided to take the leap and sailed to America.

Micho, leaving his wife and infant son behind, decided to do the same thing. As millions has done previously, he placed all his possessions in a steamer trunk, converted his Italian money into dollars, and traveled steerage class to America, landing in Boston with his trunk and twelve US dollars in his pocket.

The Gangi family who had left Sicily before him, had found a cold water flat in a growing section of a Sicilian enclave in Lawrence, Massachusetts.

The sweat shops of Lawrence, then an Industrial Revolution power house, had plenty of work for cheap laborers.

Cramming into the small apartment, he began to work in one of those sweatshops; laboring there until he was able to send for his wife.

Thomas was left in Sicily until enough money could be raised for his passage. Relatives who remained there looked after him.

Micho and the Gangi cousins scrimped and saved and decided to open a small grocery store on Common Street in Lawrence, where most Sicilians lived.

Not afraid of hard work, they worked day and night and soon the tiny business grew and Micho was able to send for his son from Sicily. Soon thereafter, he and Concetta began growing their family anew.

Another four sons and a daughter were born in the following years. In all, Gaetano and Concetta had five sons and a daughter...a big family considering his modest and humble start in life.

In America, where the streets were said to be paved with gold, this was the way.

Hard work, more hard work, and more hard work still. Save your money, sacrifice, and good things will happen. "No one ever died of hard work" became the family mantra.

As time passed, he bought out the Gangi family's share of the grocery business from his cousins, and around the time of the First World War, built his first apartment building in a partnership with his brother in law.

By age 38, he was a landlord.

He built his family a house next, and soon after another apartment building. Rumor has it that his wine making skills that he learned in Sicily came in handy ...especially during Prohibition...and the extra money earned from bootlegging *vino* really helped.

As the years passed and his children grew, they prospered. The sons all worked hard, and hard work found success for them.

Hard work was the key.

So was the doing of good deeds for people: "Do good and forget it, do bad and regret it," he would say.

His sons and daughter learned the lessons taught by Micho very well.

He died in 1959 after living a good life. When he died, his family had grown to be one of the most prominent families in the area. Nine flower cars followed the hearse to the family burial ground loaded with beautiful floral arrangements. Everyone loved and respected Micho.

After his death, his sons found account books from his Depression era grocery store that he had operated. During the Depression, hundreds of families were issued "credit" by him…money that was never collected. Thousands of dollars…in those days a king's ransom…forgiven by him.

On his tombstone it simply reads: Gaetano Torrisi 1885-1959.

The hyphen between the date of his birth and the date of his death is what is important in life, I think.

He had the guts to pick up and leave his homeland and against all odds survived and prospered.

He instilled in this family the concept of "family first," a concept which still rules his descendents to this day.

His story isn't a new story. As a matter of fact, it has been repeated millions of times in the last century by Sicilians forced to leave Sicily for America, Australia, and South America.

However, to me the story of Micho is special. Micho was my grandfather. Gaetano Torrisi, the father of my mother.

Many of his children were wildly successful in life. Many of his grandchildren and now his great grandchildren are now wildly successful.

Tens of thousands of people can point to Micho, his sons and daughter, his grand sons and grand daughters, and now his great grand sons and grand daughters… as people who helped them, employed them, counseled them, inspired them, taught them and changed their lives in some way.

Through Micho, many were touched.

If you trace all these things back to the source, if you invert the pyramid, so to speak…at the bottom of this story is an eighteen year old with a steamer trunk and twelve bucks in his pocket who came to America in search of a better life.

Gaetano Torrisi.

I bet you have your own Gaetano Torrisi in your family, right? All of them are my heroes.

His story is that of hundreds of thousands of Sicilians who left Sicily during the early twentieth century to come to America searching for a better life. They are my heroes. I bet they are your heroes too.

Some customs never change.

Take for example the Italian festivals in America.

Many of them are directly related to festivals held in Italy and Sicily.

The Fisherman's Festival, The Festival Of Santa Rosalia, Saint Anthony's Festival, Saint Joseph's Festival, The Feast of The Three Saints, are just a few of the hundreds held throughout the United States that are linked directly to Italy.

People love these festivals and generations of Italian-Americans and Sicilian-Americans have passed down these traditions to the little ones who themselves have passed it down to their little ones.

Some parade statues of their patron saints through the streets of their neighborhoods. Others have full-blown street festivals, and the streets are festooned with lights and decorations. Others try to replicate exactly the particular festivals held in their ancestral villages, towns or cities in Italy.

Back when I was a youngster (a long, long time ago), my mom told me a story of something that happened to her when she was a child.

In those days (we are talking the 1930s here), when the statues of The Three Saints (Alfio, Cirino, Filadelfo) were pulled around the neighborhood in Lawrence Massachusetts, on the main festival street, Common Street, which was the very street that the original Sicilian immigrants once lived in cramped apartments while they worked in the sweatshops. One tradition was to string wires across the street and a child, who was dressed as an angel would "fly" across the street, hooked up to a corset beneath her angel clothes.

Men on both sides of the street would construct an elaborate pulley system and "pull" the child across the street, often stopping in front of the "vara" (The wagon on which the statues of the saints were displayed and pulled by the faithful) to sing a song or say a prayer.

To have your child picked as an angel was a great honor. The event would be talked about for months afterwards, and a lot of "wrangling" would take place prior to the "big event" over which child would be picked.

Well, thanks to some arm-twisting one year by my grandfather Gaetano, my mom was chosen as the angel.

For many weeks my grandmother worked on the angel costume, and my mom, who was seven years old at the time, spend many days memorizing the prayer that she was to recite and the song she was to sing when she arrived in front of the vara after getting pulled by the ropes across the street in mid-air.

My mom, looking like a cherub and angel in her beauty, stepped out of a window from a second floor apartment on Common Street in Lawrence and the roar of the crowd was deafening as she was pulled across the street.

Until she got stuck mid-way. The pulley had stopped working!

Seems that one of the "men" who was responsible for that elaborate pulley system that would allow mom to "fly" had a little too much vino that day, and had crossed the ropes and pulleys.

Poor mom was stuck dangling half way across the street, up two stories in the air.

In no time, she was crying, screaming and kicking as the crowd below gasped in horror.

Men extended their arms trying to catch mom in case the ropes snapped and there was general pandemonium everywhere.

Fortunately, my grandfather Gaetano, a resourceful man if there was ever was one, ran up to the apartment and fixed the pulley system before disaster occurred. The father had in fact saved his "angel"

Mom, pretty shook up over this turn of events, finally arrived at the appointed spot where she sang her song and recited her prayer through tear-stained lips. The crowd roared with delight.

Of course, beside cheering, many claimed that a "miracle" had taken place. As far as I can see though, the only miracle that occurred was that of my grandfather not throttling his drunken friend!

Years later, people were still coming up to mom to remind her of that fateful day.

Mom had her own opinion of that day. "I had nightmares for weeks afterwards and peed my pants" she said. "Dumb idea that nannu had"

Oh well.

The tradition was discontinued years later and today pigeons and balloons are released instead. However, the drinking of wine still continues to this day, thank God. See? Some traditions never change!

That First Thrill
and the Last Good-Bye

No matter where you are flying from, the trip to Sicily is a long flight. There is simply no getting around it.

I often suggest to first time visitors that they consider breaking up the trip into two days ...especially if health, age, or fatigue is an issue.

Flying into Rome or Milan and spending the first night there is a nice thing to do. You can depart the next day to Sicily. This gives you an opportunity to get your body adjusted to the time change, plus you are much fresher when you arrive in Sicily.

Generally, flights leave from Rome or Milan to Catania almost hourly, so have your travel agent book a flight for you for a mid- day departure if you decide to break up the trip into two days. Another benefit of breaking up the trip is that way you can spend a couple of hours in the morning sight seeing in Rome or Milan, which is a wonderful way to start a trip.

Or, you can just fly right through and go directly to Sicily.

Depending on the time of year and how I feel, I have gone both ways (a stopover in Rome for a night or catching that connecting flight a couple hours after arriving in Rome just to get the flight over with).

I unwind on the plane from my hectic life in America. Flying is relaxing and enjoyable, so I don't mind flying straight through to Catania.

No matter how I fly, the best feeling in the world for me is the plane's approach into the Catania airport.

Once I see those volcanic islands off the Sicilian coast and later the Sicilian landscape as the plane begins banking around the Island to begin its decent, I feel elated.

I feel like I am coming home, and no matter how many times I fly to Sicily, the feeling is the same: excitement, happiness, joy and wonder.

Really, as that plane approaches Fontanarossa Airport in Catania, I feel like a child again on Christmas morning that cannot wait to open all the Christmas presents.

The excitement of the arrival is truly overwhelming. You will have so many different thoughts and feelings going through your mind and body

Mt. Etna...Europe's oldest and most active volcano. Here is a first glimpse as the plane starts its decent into Fontanarossa Airport.

that you will have a difficult time processing them all.

The first glimpse of Etna from the air on that descent (especially on a clear day) is awe-inspiring ....it will take your breathe away.

Arriving at the airport you will have a hard time not wanting to just jump in the air and click your heels with joy, believe me!

Make sure that once you land and de-plane, you know where to go and pick up your luggage. Now that passengers are restricted to only one checked bag without being charged a ridiculous amount of money, I recommend that you take a carry on bag stuffed with a couple days worth of clothing...just in case your suitcase is delayed.

Purchase a carry on that rolls. This way you won't be lugging a heavy bag all over the place. Thus you should take with you one bag that you check, and one carry on piece that rolls.

Remember go to the "International Arrival Section" and not the domestic section to pick up your bag. If you don't pay attention, you will be waiting at the wrong place all day! You will then have to clear Italian customs (called *Dogana*), which should not be a problem, provided you are carrying nothing illegal.

Then head toward the exit doors.

The effect of actually BEING in Sicily will begin to envelop you as you exit those doors.

YOU ARE IN SICILY NOW! YOU MADE IT!

For most, this is a dream come true.

From this point on, visual and audio overload will hit you. Sights, sounds...strangely different yet oh so lovely fill your eyes and ears.

Italian and Sicilian conversations now surround you. See the espresso bar to the right? You are here! Pinch yourself!

Look at the people that you see. Look at them closely. Some of them actually look like Italian people that you know back in the states!

While tourists from other parts of Europe will be arriving too, focus on the locals...the Sicilians...your people.

Enjoy your first arrival. It is a once in a lifetime experience.

Once you exit the terminal, observe the explosion of colors around you...palm trees, flowers, the texture of the landscape, the smell of the Sicilian air, the feel of the climate...the euphoria of **JUST BEING THERE** is profoundly overwhelming.

Visitors to Sicily are there either on an organized tour or are renting an auto on their own, or have friends or relatives waiting for them at the airport.

Each experience is unique.

I have witnessed many first reunions at the terminal over the years between relatives that have choked me up, truth be told.

I have witnessed many people rushing into each other's arms, weeping with joy.

I have witnessed old men who have been away from Sicily for many years or first time Sicilian Americans fulfilling a dream literally get down on a knee and kiss the ground.

Others simply thank God that He granted them their wish.

Really, that airport arrival is an overwhelming emotional experience for first time visitors.

No matter where you are driving to from the airport or in which direction, you will feel like you are in a daze...a surreal feeling that your brain is struggling to process.

Enjoy the feeling. You have earned it.

If you are flying straight through from the states, I recommend that you try to stay up as late as possible that first night…try to go to bed at nighttime instead of arriving at your destination and hitting the bed.

Taking a nap is fine, showering and changing your clothes is a great idea too, but try to last as long as you can that first day in Sicily.

The second day, you will be fine and you will hit the ground running.

Conversely, a couple of days before you have to leave Sicily, an uneasy twinge of sadness begins to form in your stomach.

Like watching a wonderful movie hoping that it never ends, you begin to dread your departure day. You wish that you can freeze time.

You wish that you can hit the replay button and start all over.

These feelings are the polar opposite of those you felt on your arrival, aren't they?

Just remember that Sicily isn't going to melt when you leave… and that you can always return… that will make you feel better, much better.

For many, that first visit has been a voyage of discovery. For many, it will stay in their hearts forever.

As you board the plane for your departure, take one last look at the Sicilian landscape.

Look at the ground below as the plane begins its ascent. Glance at Etna one last time.

Then close your eyes and promise yourself that you're coming back

That's what I always do. I'm coming back. I'm coming back to my home again…real soon.

There are a lot of "firsts' in my life that are stenciled in my mind's eye.

If I took the time and listed all the "firsts" that I have experienced in life, then I would have to change the name of this chapter, wouldn't I?

No, this chapter is about my first culinary trip to Nirvana...my first plate of pasta in Sicily.

I am not talking about a "normal" plate of pasta either. Rather, I am talking something more exotic, more unforgettable.

I am talking about a Hall Of Fame plate of pasta.

Growing up in a Sicilian-American household, eating pasta was a way of life with my family.

On Monday nights it was pasta and sauce. On Tuesday night it was pasta and peas. On Wednesday nights it was pasta and eggplant. On Thursday nights it was pasta and broccoli. You get the picture.

Every night there was pasta "primu" followed by a meat, fish or fowl "secunnu".

The only exception to this was on Sunday when mom made the traditional Sicilian "sugu" which had meatballs, chicken, sausages, and beef in it, and that pretty much was the meal. First you ate the pasta and sauce and then you ate the meat afterwards.

During Lent, mom would make special pasta and fish stew that was always one of my favorites, but she had to be really motivated to make that. Usually during Lent it was pasta with anchovy and bread crumbs... *pasta c'anciovi e muddica*...and that was it.

Thus, I considered myself a pasta expert of sorts and probably tasted every variety of pasta and sauce and every individual cut of pasta there was sometime in my life.

Before I tell you about that truly "first" great plate of pasta though, I must say that my family was a "sauce" or a "sugu" family.

In my house, "gravy" was something brown that was put on turkeys on Thanksgiving. Not red and made with tomatoes.

In America, great linguistic discussion takes place between New Englanders, New Yorkers and folks from New Jersey about the correct name

My Italian law partner avv. Massimo V. Grimaldi and his wife Anna Privitera enjoying a fine meal in Catania. Massimo and I have had many excellent adventures together over the years.

of sauce, but since the Pilgrims landed here in Massachusetts, we feel we were given the right somewhere in the Constitution…on the back page I think…to decided how to pronounce things and which words to use. Thus, I will use the term pasta "sauce" under that right.

That said, I can now proceed with my story.

I remember my first real plate of pasta as if it was yesterday. It wasn't your every day run of the mill plate of pasta, either. No, it was an exotic plate. A special plate. A plate that would have launched a thousand ships if it had been kidnapped to Troy like Helen. We are talking a seriously good plate of pasta here. We are talking here a plate of pasta of biblical proportions.

The place where we ate (no… devoured is more like it) this "Plate Meant for the Gods" of pasta was of course, in Catania.

In America, if anyone but the most proficient attempted to make this dish of pasta, the page in the Constitution referenced above requires the immediate deportation of that person on the theory of Pasta Heresy.

The restaurant in Catania is called "Il Gabbiano." It is a fish restaurant.

Usually, fish restaurants in Catania have all the fish that they will cook that evening on ice under a display case. You pick out the fish that you want, and they prepare it.

I had talked to Anna, Massimo's lovely wife, earlier in the day who taught me how to select the proper fish. In Sicily, fish usually is served head and all and it get filleted only if you specifically ask. Otherwise, you do it yourself.

"The eyes, Alfred, the eyes" I was told. "Pick a fish that has moist eyes. That means the fish is fresh. If the eyes are dried out, that means it's yesterday's fish," she said.

Yesterday's fish? Didn't she realize that most fish in America is weeks, maybe months old in any supermarket? Most of our stuff is caught and frozen, then defrosted and sold.

Only the freshest of fish markets break this rule in America. In Sicily, EVERYTHING is fresh.

This night, however, what I was eating didn't require that I examine the eyes.

It was cuttlefish.

Cuttlefish is actually a misnomer. Cuttlefish are technically mollusks... highly intelligent invertebrate...we call them squid or octopus...the point here is, the whole "examine the eye" thing doesn't work with a cuttlefish. You just have to believe the waiter when he tells you that it was just caught today. Eating this meal requires a little faith in mankind.

In any case, I had heard about this particular restaurant and its specialty, pasta con nero di seppia...pasta with cuttlefish... served with its "ink" made right into a delicious sauce.

A cuttlefish evidently has a sack of black ink that it squirts as a defense mechanism at his enemies in the sea, but this sack of ink taste wonderful when made with a red sauce.

The result is a sauce that is black...or dark jet blue. Truly amazing in taste and texture.

Il Gabbiano is the best restaurant in Catania for preparing this meal, so I naturally ordered a plate of its fabled "pasta con nero di seppia" and passed on all the other dead fish in the case that night. A bottle of white "vino bianco locale" was ordered with the meal as well.

The plate of nero di seppia was served over linguine.

No self respecting Sicilian would ever put cheese on a fish dish, and I certainly wasn't going to either.

The visual presentation of the dish was formidable: Dark black, small pieces of cuttlefish mixed right in, an intense bouquet. An unforgettable bouquet. An intoxicating bouquet.

As I placed that first forkful of pasta in my mouth, within a second, all previous memory of pasta that I had stored in my brain somehow instantaneously got deleted and I knew that this dish of pasta would be the benchmark dish of pasta that I would forever measure all others.

That dish of pasta eaten that night at Il Gabbiano Ristorante in Catania singularly is the best plate of pasta that I ever have eaten in my life.

Fresh pineapple for desert and a lemon *sorbetto* finished off a memorable meal. My companions that evening, Massimo and Anna, also were duly impressed.

Since that day, I have eaten nero di seppia many times. No matter how delicious the plate, that first dining experience has never been replicated.

I shouldn't really say that.

Because if you have never tasted Pasta Alla Norma…THE signature dish of Catania made with grilled eggplant…you have never lived either… especially topped with a nice ricotta salata cheese.

However, that was my SECOND dish of pasta that I ate the following night, and…as they say….a man can only have one first!

A. Summer

August in Sicily.

That phrase makes the air conditioner people weep with joy.

Seriously, if you like heat, then Sicily is for you in August.

How hot is it? Ever see a flock of pigeons walk? I have. Too hot to fly.

The brilliant sunshine, the African-like temperature, is negated somewhat only in the mountains of Etna…where many Italians from the North own vacation homes.

Along the coasts, beaches are packed with Sicilians, Italians, everyone really…who come to Sicily to frolic in the warm Sicilian waters and catch a breeze every now and again.

Gelato is consumed by the boatful in August. Gelato…just looking at the word waters the mouth, doesn't it?

Also consumed in great quantity is "granita" that icy concoction created by the Arabs in the eleventh century during their occupation of Sicily when they took snow from the top of Etna and put fruit flavorings in it…very similar to "Italian Ices" or "slush" found in the states…except one hundred times better. With a brioche…truly an amazing treat!

The heat heals.

It is a dry heat, similar to that in Arizona. If you are like me and have a cranky shoulder, ankle or hand due to arthritis, this is the time of the year for you.

As soon as I arrive in Sicily during this time of year, every ache and pain in my body goes away. That dry heat does wonders. I feel like I am eighteen years old again!

Heat brings mosquitoes too. Those dreaded little creatures that can disturb even the deepest sleeper as they buzz around the bed.

Woe is you if you leave a window open during the night without a screen on it. They will dive-bomb you all night. I have netting on my windows, but these little guys still find a safe place to land and snack.

I think they like American food the best.

Sunscreen? Sure …bring plenty and make sure that it is between a

Summertime in Sicily is fun time!

thirty block and a sixty block. If you are fair-skinned, this is an absolute necessity or else you will get burned to a crisp in no time flat!

However hot the Sicilian day is, at night it can be lovely. Cooling breezes sweep off the waters offering a needed respite.

The best thing of all during the summer, however, is the romance ... whether you are eight or eighty, there is nothing like a nice café or restaurant overlooking the moonlit sea...truly remarkable.

Heat in Sicily.

To truly live, you must experience it. Just make sure the air conditioning works though!

B. Fall

Fall in Sicily is my favorite time of the year. Fall starts towards the end of September and continues until about the first week of November.

I usually point to this time of the year when folks ask what months I like best or when they should visit.

August is scorching hot and sometimes the first two weeks of Sep-

Fall in Sicily is harvest time....especially the fichidindia!

tember are very hot too. By the third week of September, however, the weather calms down a little and is just perfect for touring, going to the beach, hiking, actually doing just about anything except skiing.

For me, fall also means harvest time.

The roadside farm stands are packed with farmers selling their crops of fresh figs, *fichid'india* (called "prickly pears" in America), mushrooms, all sorts of green leafy vegetables, and other delicious things that will make your mouth water.

Local communities have special events that occur at this time of the year that are wonderful to experience. The beautiful Etna hill town of Zafferana dell'Etna has its annual October Fest every weekend featuring all the items that that area is noted for, particularly honey, cordials made from lemons, pistachios, almonds, wine, hazelnuts, carob, and various types of salami and sausages.

The streets of Zafferana are lined with vendors offering samples of their products and you can have a wonderful time wandering around tasting everything. Be careful not too sample too many of the cordials though!

On the other side of the island, I do not think there is a finer experience that to have a pizza or something to eat at a restaurant overlooking the Valley of the Temples in the Agrigento area. The direction of the setting sun as it hits the Greek ruins will leave an indelible impression on your mind.

In Trapani and the central part of the island, especially the Greater Palermo area, the beginning of November signals the start of the olive harvest...which continues during the first two weeks of the month.

I have been fortunate to have witnessed many a harvest and have watched the making of olive oil by the pressers.

Every region has a centrally located olive processing facility where a grower brings his harvest and gets it pressed into oil. Most small growers, of course, sell their crop to large oil producers. For Sicily's economy, this is crucially important to them.

In Siracusa, the same thing occurs at this time of year. There, the olives are a different variety from those on the other side of the island. In Siracusa, the olive oil is more "fruity" with notes of the landscape in its bouquet. Back during the Roman occupation, the olives of Buccheri (part of greater Siracusa) were considered to be so valuable that they were used as trading currency.

In greater Messina, this time of year is perhaps the best of all. The regional pastries made from the local harvest are featured everywhere. Ceramic makers and artists fill the nooks and crannies of many villages displaying there wares.

Fall in Sicily is a celebration of life and a showing of thanks and gratitude by her people for the Islands bounty.

Fall in Sicily. It has to be experienced at least once in your lifetime.

C. Winter

Winter is Sicily means a lot of things to me. I have been fortunate to spend many holiday seasons in Sicily the past decade or so, especially over Christmas and New Year.

I much prefer the "authentic" holiday feeling in Sicily to that in America (although I have to tell you that every year, more and more commercialism is creeping into the mainstream culture).

To me, that period of time is truly special.

Sicilians really get excited about the weather this time of year...especially if it dips below fifty degrees. This is practically flip-flop and shorts weather in New England, but Sicilians drag out their winter coats, hats and mittens and grumble how cold it is. People look at me strangely and shake their heads as they see me walk by in sandals and shorts but seriously...hats and mittens?

"Brutto tempo" (terrible weather) is said by everyone. I laugh when I hear people complain. They should experience shoveling a driveway once in their lives to truly appreciate the weather!

Is there snow in Sicily? Sure. On Mt. Etna. Did you know that people actually ski on Etna in the winter?

Just seeing a white-capped Etna is a profoundly moving experience for me, and every year as I drive by a certain vista that shows her beauty, I stop my car to admire her elegance.

Sometimes, it **IS** cold in Sicily...especially since the vast majority of homes there are not insulated.

On a cold and damp rainy day, the weather **IS** miserable and a sweater is needed as well as an extra blanket on the bed.

I love the winter food however. It placates my soul.

I love eating a nice bowl of that hearty fish stew made from salted cod called "stucco"...made with re-hydrated cod or fresh cod, olives, potatoes, tomatoes and is made as a thick soup. Some regions make the stucco fish-style with a heavy sauce over the baked fish. Either way, I love eating it in the winter time..

Traveling to the central portions of Sicily during this time of year is a desolate experience. The central portion of the Island always seem colder that the coastal areas. The landscape is asleep for the winter and the crops are not yet growing.

The trade off, however, is that if you are there to visit a certain place or tourist attraction, the usual swarms of people are not there. Bargains abound everywhere. If you like to shop, then Palermo or Catania is for you as both cities offer big "sconto" (discount) every January.

La festa della Befana in January and La festa di San Valentino in February help pass the time and once March arrives, spring has arrived.

Of course, if you like to socialize, the restaurants and pizzerias are packed with locals every weekend, and the winter is probably the best time to people watch Sicilians in their native habitat.

Winter in Sicily is completely different than the other seasons, but it is still much more enjoyable than shoveling my driveway back home. A lot more enjoyable, actually.

D. *Spring*
Spring is a time of re-birth in Sicily.
It starts off with a bang and gathers steam as it progresses.
In early March, Sicilians make a big deal over "Carnevale"...especially

in Acireale, Taormina, Agrigento, Palermo, Trapani and Sciacca. Huge city wide festivals and parades kick off the Lent season and "Mardi Gras" or "Carnevale" as they say in Sicily is a wonderful time. Five weeks later, the Easter season starts, and Easter in Sicily is a "can't miss".

Actually the Good Friday processions all over the Island are a "can't miss"…as the fight of good versus evil is highlighted in art, theater, and in processions. This day is a truly remarkable day in Sicily. Profoundly sad and profoundly religious.

Three days later, the Easter celebration sits at the extreme opposite of emotion. The Risen Christ is celebrated and everywhere friends and family gather to celebrate the holiday.

If you are an artist, spring in Sicily is for you, as the explosion of colors, sights and sounds will inspire your greatest work. Stop by any countryside vista and you will see amazing mixtures of reds, greens, pinks, purples, and browns as the Sicilian countryside springs back to life.

Spring in Sicily is when I make my annual pilgrimage to my ancestral hometown of Trecastagni and pay homage to my three patron saints Alfio, Filadelfo, and Cirino…three boys who were martyred by the ancient Romans for refusing to give up their Christian faith sixteen hundred years ago. I now plan my entire month of May around this two day festival.

Spring also means a trip to Pachino, way down at the southeastern tip of the Island to eat at the best fish restaurants in Sicily. Grilled prawns are always ordered and eaten by me on this annual trip to fish heaven, and no trip there would be complete without eating the fabled cherry tomatoes of Pachino.

Cefalù is wonderful in the spring too, as the artist and street sellers return and the beautiful town springs to life. Throughout Sicily…no matter where you go…its annual re-birth is ongoing and the May-June period of spring is perhaps the finest of all.

Summer, fall, winter and spring…four unique and different textures and feelings in one magical place.

Amazing.

Some things in America we take for granted. Running water, heat, electricity and the telephone.

In Sicily, you never know what to expect.

As usual I departed for Sicily last Christmas Day and was one exhausted camper.

The year had been a tough year for me (and for all of America for that matter...the economy was getter worse by the minute).

I counted the days leading up to my departure, working day and night trying to get ahead of the game.

With my busy schedule and responsibilities at two law schools, promoting my book "The Reverse Immigrant," and then trying to do all the "normal" Christmas stuff, by the time I was ready to leave for Sicily, I was out of gas.

Exhausted.

I had booked a flight thru Delta this time. Delta code shares with Alitalia and it was cheaper booking thru them than it was booking directly thru Alitalia.

Geez.

No wonder that Alitalia is broke. I saved four hundred dollars for a ticket on the same plane, plus I got my Alitalia miles at check-in too! Good businessmen those Italians, no?

The plane was full of Italians and Americans going to Rome. Thankfully the trip was on an Airbus (more leg room in economy) and the guy sitting next to me was skinny. This meant that I wouldn't be a sardine this time. Usually on the trip over, I have to fold my legs and stuff them in my shirt pocket for the flight, but this time there was actually some room for me to move around and breathe a little.

Usually, I never eat the food onboard. I only eat what I can identify, so that means I don't eat the Alitalia offerings. One time the flight attendant asked me "Fish or meat?" as she was serving dinner. I told her meat. Thus, I was surprised when I opened up that little container and found chicken inside. Getting her attention, I nicely told her that she had given me chicken instead of meat. She told me "chicken is meat."

Lesson learned.

Now, I bring something with me. Usually a salad, some trail mix… nothing heavy. About the worst possible thing that can happen to a human being on a long haul flight to Europe is having to use the restrooms during a flight.

Don't.

Especially "don't" after the plane has been in the air several hours. As the flight attendants are gabbing away and reading magazines during the flight, you would think that every once in a while they would at least check the hygiene of the rest rooms. They don't. Woe is you have to use a rest room twenty minutes before landing.

Better still, woe is you if turbulence hits the plane and you are still in the restroom! Woe triply to you if you are a man standing up in the restroom while turbulence hits. Close your eyes a second and enjoy that visual. THAT'S WHY I try not to use the restrooms.

Of course, that explains why I also try to rush out of the plane as soon as it lands. "Holding it in" and "running off the plane" are related in that context, I think.

I do, however, drink the wine on board.

Fortunately, Alitalia offered a nice wine from Apulia on the flight, so I usually have one glass or two.

Then I zonk out.

In any case, the next thing I knew I was in Rome.

Eight hours of a wine-induced sleep. Hey, when in Rome do as the Romans do, right?

Last Christmas' flight was the shortest flight over I can ever remember, there I was …in Rome…after what seemed to be a two hour flight. It was really an eight hour flight, but six hours of sleep really helped.

As usual, the airport in Rome was deserted Christmas morning.

Which I love.

My IPOD was on by this time and strolling thru the nearly empty terminal (after I have hit the restroom) is now a tradition for me. The "tight as a drum" feeling that I have in America began to fade and a new persona took root in me. My Sicilian persona.

I hit my favorite spot in Terminal B for espresso, cornetti and some fruit and do what I love to do best at the airport: watch people.

This was a Bob Marley type of day. Listening to him, then listening to a little Average White Band (vintage stuff), and wandering around the terminal while I waited for my connecting flight to Catania, I observed very interesting folks.

I struck up a conversation with a woman heading to meet her husband in Sicily who was stationed at Sigonella Navy Base. She was from Mississippi. She had never left Mississippi before....This was her first international flight and she was relieved to find a friendly face who knew where to go in such a big airport. She told me that she had been married for just five months before her husband had been deployed to Sicily. She was joining him for a three year tour of duty there.

Two other gals overhead us talking in English and joined the conversation.

One was a professional runner from the US Olympic team who was going to Sicily to meet her boyfriend. Another was a Navy wife.

Thus, I spent my time in Rome baby-sitting three very attractive women who all were on their maiden flights to Sicily.

Hmm. I thought. This may be the beginning of a very memorable trip. I liked the early omens.

Arriving in Sicily, we said our good-byes, (although the three waiting men looked at me suspiciously at first), they all thanked me when their women informed them that I had guided them safely.

Picking up my car (a standard five gear Peugeot) at the car rental agency (an agency that I will never use again...later in the book I describe that experience), I threw my stuff in the car and zipped off.

The only foul-up so far was that I had noticed that my Italian passport had expired. It wasn't a big deal. I was traveling this time on my US passport, but still meant that I had to go to Boston and get a new one when I returned, as I was planning on declaring residency in Sicily on my next trip back in several months and I wanted everything in apple pie order.

Italian passports are good for five years, not ten years as the American passport. I had forgotten.

Arriving in Acitrezza, I opened the front door to my condo. I was home (finally) and was very happy. I thanked the Good Lord for the ten thousandth time for my good fortune and entered my place.

My caretakers had done a good job. Fresh linens. Condo clean. They even set up a Christmas display.

Nice touch.

In any case, I was in desperate need of food and a shower.

Stripping naked, I jumped in the shower and waited for the hot water.

It never came.

No hot water.

Crap.

I then had to use the classic Sicilian method of taking a shower when the water heater won't work: First I got three big pans of water. Then I put them on the stove. Then I heated them up. Then I took each of them to the bathroom. Then I put them on a chair. Then I stepped in the shower. With a wash cloth I covered myself in soap lather. Finally, one at a time, I poured the three pans of water over me to wash away the grime and soap.

I washed the whale.

Successfully.

You didn't think a little cold water was going to stop me, did you?

Since December 26th is also a holiday in Sicily, that means on the 27th I had to address the problem. Two days of showering this way. At this point, I just wanted to make sure that I got the problem fixed by the time I went home......which was in two weeks!

In any case, I was home...and slowly I could feel myself relaxing... and becoming human again.

Thank God.

I am amazed that each and every time that I return to this place the same set of feelings hit me: profound happiness that I am here, profound joy that the Lord has given me yet another opportunity to experience something wonderful, and profound amazement at what I see and experience.

To me, just unlocking that condo door is the best Christmas present that I could possible get.

Home again.

Such a beautiful yet such a dirty city.

All it would take is a little elbow grease to clean this town up and make it into Sicily's show piece, but that will never happen, I think.

Politics.

Politics keeps this city hostage…and dirty …and I can't understand it.

Don't the folks there realize that a clean city will attract a lot more tourists?

Not the whole city is dirty. The central tourist area around the Duomo and Corso Sicilia are in decent shape. The port isn't in bad shape either. The rest of the city needs a good cleaning.

When politics rears its ugly head, watch out!

For years, garbage pick-up has been used as a political tool in some parts of Italy and Catania is a close second to Naples in this regard. Naples ALWAYS has garbage problems. Catania ONLY has garbage problems when an election is around the corner.

When the Right is in power (as it is now), left leaning unions strike at the slightest thing…usually in sympathy with other unions.

When that happens with the garbage guys, all hell breaks loose.

In Sicily, people put their garbage (supposedly) in huge plastic bins located on every block for the garbage men to take away. No one has trash barrels in Sicily. A set tax is assessed on everyone (usually about 200 euro a year) and plastic bins are set up on every block so the residents can throw their trash away. Then the trash men come around and empty the bins.

Or so it should be in theory.

Allegedly, they have bins to re-cycle glass, plastic and paper, but other than the college kids and young adults, re-cycling hasn't yet hit the Sicilian consciousness.

Thus the theory of efficient collection of trash often crashes and burns.

When those bins get full, people still keep throwing their garbage in the general direction of where they THINK the trash bin is, and every once in a while you will see a huge mountain of trash littered on, over, beside and in between these overflowing bins.

Worse, people here generally do not buy those green Hefty Trash Bag type garbage bags that we use.

They use the plastic bags that they get when they go shopping… grocery store bags. The small white ones. They "re-cycle" in this manner: use the plastic white trash bag and overfill it with thrash until it almost is bursting, then throw it in the trash bins, where, of course, it breaks open and spills trash all over the place.

Moreover, often people don't even bother to stop their car and put their trash IN the bins. Some people simply slow down their cars, open their window and throw that garbage in the general direction of the trash bin.

Some time it goes in, most times it ends up on the ground.

Sicilians are not basketball players, unfortunately, and their aim stinks.

Then again, so does the garbage.

As a result, places have the mangiest cats hanging out at these bins… one eyed tom cats that look mean. They tear open the bags on the ground and pretty soon there is a mess everywhere.

If Catania ever decides to fix this problem (believe me, every day there is a story in the newspaper about this issue, and many people complain),

The elephant….Catania's symbol.

then I will say that Catania is beautiful.

However, until that day, I will not. It is dirty city that needs to be cleaned up.

I noticed this year that Sicilian supermarkets are phasing out plastic garbage bags and encouraging their customers to use cloth bags. Sooner or later, this will catch on, as will re-cycling. When it does, then a big step toward a cleaner Catania will be accomplished.

The downtown area, however, IS beautiful. When it is all spiffed up, it is amazing, actually.

Norman and Spanish castles are everywhere. The city...built almost all in lava rock has a baroque feel to it. Black and brown lava rock and white sandstone combine to make many a beautiful building.

The Duomo (The city's main Cathedral) in the center of town is really beautiful. Corso Sicilia (the main thoroughfare) has elegant shops, cafes, restaurants. The museums are interesting (not great) and the Fish Market and Port are outstanding. The British Cemetery located by the airport which is the resting place for 8,000 British soldiers killed during the Second World War, is a testimony to British sacrifice. It inspires me every time I visit this sacred place.

However, I always advise tourists not to go to Catania at night unless they know exactly where they are going or they are escorted by someone who knows where they are going, because it can be a little dangerous.

Kids on motor bikes... who can spot a rental car's license plate a mile away....will try to open your car door and snatch a handbag.

One night when my son Matt was with me a few years ago, some kids tried to cut off our car in order to rob us. They were teenagers, no more that 16 or 17. They pulled alongside and then drove ahead of us and cut us off.

Behind us, two kids in a motor bike approached. My son Matt and I briefly talked about getting out of the car to break their necks...after all Matt is tough as nails and I have been in a scrape or fifty myself...and we wanted to show these kids how Americans handle these sort of problems.

However, after thinking about it for a few seconds, we decided that if the cops came and saw us beating these punks that we'd probably get arrested ourselves so we decided to drive the car around the idiots who had cut us off and head to the highway.

A year earlier, my cousin's wife had her purse snatched…which was holding two passports…and a lovely trip ended up being a disaster for them.

Garbage and punks aside (even Boston has punks, doesn't it?), if you stick to the tourist places when unescorted you will be fine and enjoy yourself.

However, an ounce of prevention is worth a pound of cure.

Still, Catania is a beautiful place. I only wish they would not use the trash bins as a political football and improve their aim a little!

By the way, Catania hase a wonderful *Serie* A professional soccer team and they have a rivalry with the professional *Serie* A team from Palermo that rivals any Red Sox-Yankees rivalry we have in the states. When these two teams play each other, virtually all of Sicily is glued to the TV sets.

Catania. Even though I grumble about it, I still love it.

The Feast of Santo Stefano (Saint Stephen) is a big deal in Sicily. He was the first Christian martyr according to legend.

In typical Sicilian style, the Christmas "holiday season" actually consists of the following: Christmas Eve, Christmas Day, The Feast of Santo Stefano, New Year's Eve, New Year's Day and *La festa della Befana...* it actually stretches into January.

In America, the only thing I know about Saint Stephen is that good King Wenceslas went down on his feast day. That's it. I know about him what I learned in that Christmas carol.

In Italy, the feast which is on December 26th each year, is another day off from school and work. Another in the endless list of National holidays.

It is a day when families gather and eat the left-overs from Christmas Eve and Christmas Day but for me it's just another day to mooch yet another free meal from friends.

Since I never mooch anything in America, I feel that I have accumulated all these mooch-chips over the years and am entitled to something every once in a while, namely a great meal from a great friend.

Several years back, I sponsored a young gal named Maria Pace to come to America to study English.

She stayed in my home for about ten months while she completed her course work at a nearby college, and ever since then whenever I am in Sicily she repays me by doing something nice for me. Her friendship is payment enough as I always tell her, but every time I am in Sicily we always catch up with each other.

Usually she invites me over to her family's house for a feast.

This year was different.

She fell in love with a handsome doctor from Catania named Alessio and they bought a house together in Viagrande.

Today was her first "feast" ...her mom, dad, sister, brother, nieces and nephews were coming...and Maria was cooking her first meal for them.

In Sicily, this is a BIG deal.

To her mom and sister, this would be the "final-exam" test. Kind of like the "Dancing With The Cooks" show where they would eat and subtly grade the meal simply by the look on their faces

To a Sicilian woman, a nod of the head, a raised eye brow, a small hand gesture is a signal…understood only by relatives…and Maria's mom and sister would be the ultimate graders.

Maria's mom is named Agatha and her sister is named Immacolata. Nino is Maria's father.

Nino is one great guy and he lives for his four grandchildren (the children of Maria's sister and brother). To say that he is a wonderful nannu is understating his love for those kids.

Maria had called me and told me the general vicinity of where her new place was located. I found it with no difficulty. It was right off the street by the Church of San Mauro in Via Grande and her description to me was sufficient to get there.

In America, where she lives, is called an apartment building. It was an apartment building of three floors, two apartments per floor.

In Sicily, you can buy them. Thus they are apartment-condos. Each floor owned by the occupant.

Maria was lucky. Like what's happening in America, young kids can't afford to buy a house. The banks aren't lending anything to anybody.

However, this apartment had been owned previously by Maria's grandfather who had passed on and was left to Maria's mom, uncles and aunts and siblings.

They gave her a generous price and somehow they got financing by the bank. Thus Maria was one of the very fortunate few who had home ownership while in their thirties.

On the second floor lives one aunt, on the third floor another uncle, so they succeeded in keeping the place in the extended family. In Sicily, that's the way it is.

The place was freshly painted and cheery. There were five "vani" (rooms) in all and a nice walk-out patio.

The living room was a good size for an apartment and the table was set for fourteen guests there.

Down the corridor was on one side the "bagno" (bathroom), the "cucina" (kitchen), and at the end of the hall their bedroom was on one side and an empty room across from it.

This would be for the baby Nino explained to me "If God wants."

Thus, Maria and Alessio were pretty much set for life and this was to be her first effort at entertaining the family.

Surprisingly, Nino insisted that I sit at the head of the table.

This was a great honor and I reluctantly agreed.

45

Everyone sat at their appointed places and then the appetizers that Maria had made were brought out, small slices of homemade "scacciata" (meat pie), cheese, olives, canapés, and cold-cuts.

The meat pie was delicious. Nice crusty dough baked perfectly and full of meat, cheese, olives.

Delicious. Maria hit a home run with that scacciata according to the glances of mom and her sister.

The "primu" (first course) was pasta with peas and meat in a wonderful "sugu" (meat sauce) that Maria had made the day before. It was rich, dark, and flavorful. Maria had done a great job on the "sugu."

The "secunnu" (second course) was *sasizza* (sausage) and *puppetti* (meatballs) with fresh bread, and vegetables.

Maria had done a masterful job on her first big effort, and the look on the faces of her mom and sister had confirmed my thought.

After we ate, we sat around talking politics, the economy, the children, America…while munching on cannoli and sipping the wonderful after dinner aperitif "amaro" and then espresso.

This family get together I thought to myself was probably being repeated tens of thousands of time in Italy and Sicily today.

Family.

On the Feast of Saint Stephen's Day.

Family is and will always be the central reason of existence for Sicilians. The core of the existence of virtually the entire island.

Maria's family is not rich in material terms. Straight middle class. However, they have the richness of love, and the richness of a very strong family bond.

The love and respect that I saw among her family today has no price tag, and the little ones there today were learning about love from their grandfather.

What a wonderful thing.

On the way home I thought that what I saw today is what everyone should have.

Maybe that's what Saint Stephen thought too.

Maybe we should celebrate this feast day in America too!

Car rental companies have taken renting a car in Sicily to a new level. They are now connivers of the worst kind.

I call them legal bandits.

And that goes for all the big national companies too.

Beware of the car rental companies. Here's the story:

Before leaving America, I always pre-pay for my rental car. This way, I have peace of mind upon my arrival that a car is in fact there in Sicily waiting in my name.

You are given a voucher by the travel agent that you present to the clerk at the car rental agency and the paperwork gets processed.

You need a valid license, a passport and a major credit card.

Upon arrival from Boston, after a fourteen hour travel day, I was pooped. All I wanted was my car, drive home, take a hot shower and get settled in.

At the counter, I presented my voucher, my identification and was told sign here and here, initial here and here and here are the keys.

I have to remember that from now on, no matter how tired I am, when someone tells me to sign here and here and initial here and here, I will read the entire agreement!

Why? Because I failed to read closely what I was signing, I got snookered by these legal bandits.

Here's what happened as a result:

I always check the balances on my credit cards before I leave America.

I like to have a few hundred dollars "for emergency" as extra. In Sicily I pay cash, but it is always nice to know that you have that cushion "just in case".

The next day after I had settled into the condo and went online to check the balances in my bank account and on my credit cards, to my surprise, the account showed a $650.00 charge from the car rental company!

That's odd, I thought.

I had paid for the car with another credit card in America, plus I had the voucher which I gave them when I picked up the car as proof of payment. Why the double charge?

Must me a mistake, I thought.

There was a mistake, all right, on my part.

For trusting these thieves.

Seems like car rental companies now charge an amount equal to the car rental price the card as a "security deposit" and block that amount on the card until you return the car.

To add insult to injury, buried in the fine print of that rental agreement is a box that they checked and as a result, I was charged an extra $100 for car insurance that was completely unnecessary.

Thus, this little wind up toy of a car that I had just rented cost me an extra hundred bucks plus the block of an extra $650 on my credit card.

Furious, I called customer service to complain.

The first thing that I hear is this: "Welcome to customer service. There will be a 25 cent connection charge and a five cent per minute charge to speak to a customer service representative."

Huh?

Are you kidding me?

Nope.

Not only were they ripping me off, but now they were charging me when I called to complain!

Bandits.

In any case, I got nowhere with these idiots. They gave me some cockamamie story that due to credit card fraud, this was now standard procedure, and sorry that I wasn't informed.

Seems like I was the idiot for renting a car from this outfit.

In any case, my card was blocked for double the amount and the lesson learned is this:

Either buy a car now and leave it in Sicily or rent one from an agency away from the airport.

Thankfully I had sufficient cash on hand to have a wonderful time, but as they say in the law: "Caveat Emptor" (Let the buyer beware).

Truer words were never spoken.

The Daily Grind

I thought you would be interested to learn about what I do in Sicily (beside eat, drink and be merry), so here is a rundown of a "normal" workday for me when I am here.

7:00 AM: woke up, checked emails, made coffee, sat on my deck and gazed at the Ionian Sea and got mentally prepared for a business meeting in Catania. Sitting on my deck with the spectacular view of the morning sun rising over the sea gives me pause to think: Is this the most beautiful spot in the world or what?

8:30 AM: Drove to Catania. Bumper to bumper traffic as usual. People leave later to work in Sicily than we do in America. They usually have a mid-day break from 1:30 PM to 4:00 PM, but then return to work until 8:00 PM. Thus it seems that everyone leaves for work at 8:30 AM.

I didn't mind the traffic here as much as New England because, well, I am in Sicily, and because I had a good FM station on. However, my meeting today is at the Excelsior Hotel which is located in the dead center of the city, and I was worried about finding a space to park. Finding a parking space in Catania is a nightmare. Public lots are few and far between. The concept of a parking garage is usually a foreign concept here. People just keep driving in circles it seems until they find a spot.

At every stop light, "undocumented immigrants "or "illegal aliens" (depending on if you are a liberal or conservative) approach the car and offer to wash the windows. With the recent events in Egypt, Tunisia and Libya, people seem to be flocking into the country desperate to survive, and these "window washers" are now everywhere. Not just one of them... about twelve of them will approach you. I was told to ignore them and that is what I do.

10:00 AM: Arrived at the Hotel and spend 15 euro on a decent breakfast...eggs, sausage, bacon, potato, toast, coffee and fruit. This is the only place in the city where you can get an "American" breakfast. The Excelsior is an elegant hotel and I always have my meetings there. I taught Massimo the importance long ago of "home court advantage." I never visit potential clients...they visit me. The staff, as usual, is friendly and accommodating.

Massimo and I are scheduled to meet a man from Enna who may want to hire us as consultants for his company. He manufactures various products in the Cefalù area and we are curious to meet him and see his business plan.

10:30 AM The client arrives. He is a young man 33 years old, very handsome, impeccably dressed. He has black hair, appears very suave and debonair. Most Sicilian businessmen dress this way. During the normal workday it is highly unusual for a Sicilian businessman to be without a jacket and tie. His name is Riccardo. After about 10 minutes of chit chat we get down to business. He shows us his products. Beautiful packaging and tasty products.

However, he hasn't a clue about importing requirements into America. He brought samples of marmalades, (good), nut creams (outstanding) and a line of honeys (awesome). The packaging was acceptable for Sicily but needed to be completely re-done to satisfy the American' requirements.

Getting this man's company ready for the US markets will take a lot of work, I thought…and money.

Massimo went over everything that we do (we have done this so often with businessmen here that we have our "story" down cold) and within thirty minutes, the guy realized that he needed us if he was serious about importing into America. It is far more complicated a process than to simply load products into a container and send them to America…not with the American FDA and US Customs waiting on the other end. If things were not done exactly correct, the businessman runs the risk of having his products sequestered, seized, or destroyed by US authorities.

We told him what we thought it would cost him to get his company ready for the US market and we said our good byes.

Massimo and I knew we wouldn't see this guy again. Just like most (not all) Sicilian businessmen that we meet, Ricardo simply lacked the sophistication needed to compete with other exporters.

2:30 PM: We met with some Russian businessmen who have travel agencies in Moscow and St. Petersburg and need high end clothing places locally where their rich clients can shop privately for brand names. Can we put them together with reputable people?

We had previously contacted ten high end shops from Taormina to Siracusa willing to get involved with these men and also made arrangements with a private minivan company who would cart their customers around. However, the biggest problem is finding winter clothes for their customers while they are here, which is in the summer. Russians need warm boots, coats, bags, and jackets for the cold Russian weather, not bikinis or thongs. They want to shop here in Sicily while on vacation to bring things home that they cannot find there. Sicilians do not understand that. They cannot think outside the box. Finding winter clothing outlets in Sicily that sell winter clothes in the summer will prove difficult. For all retailers, winter clothing isn't available until after the summer. This one will need a lot more research.

After this appointment both Massimo and I head home to rest up a bit. I have an evening appointment in Naxos and Massimo has to get back to the law office for other matters.

8:30 PM: Meeting with my dear friend Roberto in Naxos. He is the man. He knows everyone far and wide. If anyone can find top end winter clothing in the summer, it is my man Roberto. This guy is top shelf...the new breed of educated Sicilians who "gets it." I respect this man enormously and we are firm and fast friends.

After explaining to him the needs of the Russian businessmen, he too is concerned about acquiring a supply of winter clothing in the summer.

At best, he thinks that only last year's winter styles would be available in the summer, but the Russians were careful to tell us that they wanted current styles and not leftovers.

Alfred M. Zappala and Massimo Grimaldi....two truly unique characters in the history of the law!

Roberto also told me that there was talk of an enormous discount shopping mall that may be opening in a year or two near Taormina. Thus, we risk wasting a lot of time, effort and energy on a project that may be surpassed in two years by a huge discount mega mall outlet.

Seems like we did a lot of tire kicking today…same as any businessman does in America.

Some ideas are good, some not so good. However, as William James once said 'The essence of genius is knowing what to eliminate."

Today we eliminated a couple of business ideas that seemed appealing on first look. However, tomorrow will bring more opportunities.

For that, I am sure.

My most precious possession: a picture of my three children, Jennifer, Matthew, and Catie Rae in our ancestral village of Trecastagni.

I cannot believe how bad the education system is in Sicily regarding the teaching of the English language.

Until the day comes that Sicilians take the teaching of the English language seriously and really make an effort to get competent teachers to teach youngsters, it will languish behind almost all the other developed European Union nations.

Sicily is languishing behind because most can't speak English and we need to do something about it.

In major cities like Rome, Milan, and Florence, this is not the case. Kids speak English fairly well…because the teachers there can speak it. However, I cannot tell you how many times I have met high school English teachers in Sicily over the years that can barely speak the most rudimentary essentials of the English language.

Really, this is terrible.

Since nepotism is rampant in the hiring of teachers in Sicily, one result (among many other bad results) is that incompetent teachers who are "recommended" for the position are hired over more qualified and competent teachers. Unless you are "recommended" for a good position by a politician or a powerful person, your resume will get tossed in the garbage.

It's not what you know; rather it's who you know…unfortunately.

I remember one time back in high school in America a long time ago, I had a teacher who did not know anything about the subject he was teaching. I always believed that he was one or two pages ahead of his students in terms of preparation. If I asked him a question about a topic in the next chapter, he would have a blank expression on his face and avoid answering the question. Really, he was a joke.

Unfortunately, that is the rule rather than the exception in Sicily with regard to teaching English.

At most universities, professorships are handed down from father to son or daughter. Almost like an inheritance. As a result, many teachers are flat out incompetent or just do not care about their performance.

Not only that, but at the college level, most professors are "left" leaning ...borderline socialist or communist...to the point of flat out teaching propaganda to their students. The teaching unions are so strong that change is almost impossible. If you're in, you're in as the saying goes.

As a result, public education fails miserably in their primary task... to prepare youngsters for life.

Savvy Sicilians get their children into private schools fast, or hire English tutors for their children. A quick glance at a phone book in Palermo, Siracusa, Messina and Catania or any other urban area has many private tutoring companies who fill the gap...for a price.

I remember many times when I was at the Fancy Food Show in New York City that Sicilian businessmen...whose expenses were completely paid for by the Sicilian government...could not speak one word of English... and the one or two interpreters who could speak English were going crazy running back and forth from booth to booth trying to help these men out.

As a result, many a business deal was lost due to the language problems.

One time, I suggested to Massimo that we should put on a seminar to teach Sicilian businessmen the rudiments of business English.

"And who do you think will come, Alfred?" Massimo asked. "No one will pay anything here to learn English. It is very stupid, but true" he said.

When I point this out to Sicilians, they all agree it is a terrible thing, but strangely the situation does not change.

As a result, Sicily is stagnant...and lagging behind those countries that DO stress English.

Until this fundamental issue is addressed, Sicily will not be a world business player, heck, she won't even be a European Union player...and her young will keep leaving the Island in droves seeking employment opportunities elsewhere, which is a shame.

I would love to see an American school or three adopt a Sicilian school and get the ball rolling.

Sicily can be helped by the Americans who call her their homeland.

I really believe that. That is one way we American-Sicilians can help: Teach them to speak English.

Every little bit helps. It really does.

Cut-Throat "Setti e Mezzu"

When I was a little boy back in Lawrence, one of my favorite holiday events was playing the ancient Sicilian card games "Scupa" and "Setti e Mezzu" with my grandparents and uncles and aunts.

I have many fond memories as a youngster sitting around the dining room table with my grandparents, aunts, uncles, and cousins playing cards after a wonderful holiday dinner.

That was the tradition in our house…playing cards…Sicilian card games…after dinner.

In those days, we used an "American" deck of cards and played by removing the jacks, queens and kings. We didn't have the "real" Sicilian playing cards, so we had to make do with what we had.

I loved the playful back and forth that took place as we played. Memories of long departed loved ones and their laughter still ring in my ears. I recall those wonderful moments now lost in time and wish that we could do it again. I can still see them in my mind's eye, truth be told.

It seems that everyone forgot their troubles in life and were transported back to a simpler place for a while as they played cards.

Just like they did in Sicily.

I didn't realize how important sitting around a table and playing cards was to a Sicilian.

There are many more "serious" card games that the "men" played in those days… "zicchinetta" and "briscola" are two games that leap to mind, but for me, it was "scupa" and "setti e mezzu."

As the years past by and I got older, and as the old timers passed on, those childhood games with the family faded into the recesses of my mind.

Until last night. At Massimo's house.

After nearly fifty years, I again played "setti e mezzu"…and loved every single minute of it.

For a brief moment last night, I was transported back in time to a simpler place, a loving place that I just wish I had never left.

Massimo and Anna invited me over to their house for pizza. Massimo's sister who lives in Trieste in Northern Italy was in Sicily visiting her and Masssimo's mother Theresa for the holidays and everyone was invited over for pizza and cards.

I love Massimo's mom. She was born in Malta. She met her late husband Aldo while on holiday in Sicily fifty years ago, they fell in love, got married, and had four children.

As she told me ten thousand times "Alfred, I have lived in Sicily for fifty years, but I am Maltese."

She is also fluent in English, speaking with a slight British accent, as her school in Malta was run by the British.

Being very religious and a very devout Catholic, I often tried to draw her into a religious discussion but she never took the bait.

"Forget it, Alfred" she'd say. "Benedict is the pope. Popes can do no wrong. They speak for God."

I always sit next to Theresa at family gatherings, and last night was no exception.

In my halting Sicilian dialect, we talked about everything, and a few of the nephews joined in.

Pizza was the fare of the evening, and it was delicious. Anna had made it in the home "furno" that they have.

Afterward, we enjoyed the obligatory pantone and amaro.

Then, the air got serious.

Very serious.

It was time to play cards.

The pennies, nickels and dimes came out and everyone put on their "setti-mezzu" faces.

For the next ninety minutes the play was spirited, and everyone, young and old played.

I had forgotten the rules of the game, and initially had trouble deciphering the symbols of the cards. We were using authentic Sicilian playing cards, and there are symbols, not numbers on them.

Anna was the dealer and in short order she had a pile of pennies in front of her.

"Card shark," I thought.

I never won a single hand, which was sad because Massimo's five year old Marzio won two.

Geez.

Authentic Sicilian playing cards.

In any case, for an hour and a half last night, I was a five year old boy re-living a very happy time of my life.

After I got home, I poured myself a cognac.

Sitting on my deck, I silently toasted my grandparents.

I missed the memories of a life long forgotten. I missed the sounds of my family, especially all those long departed.

I missed my mom and dad, my two sets of grandparents, all my departed aunts and uncles. Now, me, my brother, and my sister were the family leaders, with children, nieces and nephews and grandchildren behind us now.

We are the family elders now.

As I young boy, I thought that my folks would live forever.

I never doubted their mortality.

However, tonight…just for a few moments…I remembered and re-lived a bygone time.

I remembered them all. While playing a card game in Sicily.

Gosh, what a wonderful evening.

The following is a true story. Absolutely true.

I haven't told you about my friend Rosario (Saro) Messina yet, have I?

Saro is the nicest man in the world and I love him very much. He and his wife Agatha live in Viagrande.

He is a simple man...a stone worker and we have been friends for many years.

My friend in America Peter Messina originally introduced me to him years ago when I needed help with my first house in Pachino, and we just bonded. Every time I am in Sicily, I make sure that I call him just to say hello. He is a wonderful man.

Saro works hard at his trade and that twinkle in his eye often tells of the mischievous things that he must have done in his younger days. Built like a bull, everyone in Viagrande knows and loves him. He is a generous man with a heart as big as the Island. He is a true son of Sicily.

I met him ten years ago.

I needed a driver for me and my American friends that I was with, and Peter Messina told me that Saro would be available, so I made arrangements to meet him.

From the first time we met, we became firm and fast friends.

He took me everywhere that first time. He helped me located my ancestral home in Trecastagni, he helped me find documents at town hall, he showed me how to hunt for wild porcini mushrooms on the slopes of Etna, he introduced me to everyone who was anyone in his town.

In short, Saro became one of my favorite people in all of Sicily in short order.

When I bought my first place in Pachino way down on the southeastern tip of Sicily, he was the guy who made the three hour trip with me and repaired everything. The place hadn't been used in a few years and a lot of work had to be done.

He did it all...including doing a beautiful job on the outside landscaping. In exchange, I gave him free run of the place when I wasn't in Sicily, and he often would travel down there to fish or hunt. In short, he treated that place as if it were his own.

One time, however, we had a problem.

"Alfred," he said. "I got a call from the neighbor. He told me that there is a big bee hive under the outdoor sink by your front door. Don't worry though. When we go down there tomorrow, I will fix it"

To me, bees are nothing to sneeze at. I have always been wary of bees...especially Sicilian bees that I heard stories about. I know killer bees are from South America, maybe there is a variety of Sicilian killer bee that I had never heard about? Imagine that: Sicilian killer bees. You'd really have to destroy the whole hive in order to eliminate the problem! I wouldn't want to fool around with a bee from Sicily that was mad at me!

"Ok, Saro," I said. "Tomorrow I will go with you and help you fix the problem."

Early the next day, we drove to Pachino. Saro told me that he had "the machine" to fix the problem.

I was happy. I had visions of swatting bees all night and was very nervous about the whole thing. I kept dreaming about a swarm of angry bees chasing me down a Sicilian highway stinging me on the butt, and I did not enjoy the dream one bit.

In any case, as we approached the house, we saw the biggest swarm of bees imaginable. The swarm was so big that it practically blackened the sky. I could not believe what I was seeing.

It looked like a huge funnel of black extending up in the sky for one hundred feet.

"Don't worry, Alfred" he said. "We'll wait until the queen takes them all inside, then I will fix the problem."

We watch as tens of thousands of bees made their way into this enormous hive that stood four feet high by two feet wide under my outdoor sink.

I had never seen such a monster hive in my life.

"Saro," I said. "Are you sure that you can handle this?" I said.

"Stop worrying" he said. "I'll fix the problem. Wait in the car."

Wait in the car? Why? Thinking about what he told me though, I thought that it was a good idea, and not only did I wait in the car, but I kept the motor running. I figured that if Saro got into trouble, I'd back

My house in Pachino...site of the famous "Bee Massacre!

up, get him and off we'd go.

No bees could chase down a Fiat Punto, could they?

As soon as the bees went into the hive, Saro sprung into action.

He leapt from the car and popped open the trunk.

In the trunk was a blow torch...a World War II vintage blow torch!

It must have been sixty years old! It was an old relic of a blow torch that looked like a rifle except it has an open muzzle on it.

I couldn't believe what I saw. What was he going to do?

He approached the hive (with no protective clothes on I might add) and lit that torch up. A jet stream of fire erupted from the torch.

A HUGE jet stream. A massive jet stream. Within two seconds, bees started streaming from the hive.

Saro didn't want to burn the hive. Instead, he directed the stream of fire about three feet away from the hive, scorching every bee that came out.

In five minutes, it was over. Crispy critters were everywhere. Bee corpses were all over the place.

I could not believe my eyes.

"Saro" I said "Why didn't you burn the hive?" I asked.

As I spoke those words, Saro went back to the trunk and pulled out

(l-r) Saro Messina, his cousin Peter Messina from Viagrande and Methuen, Ma., and me in from of our beach house in Pachino.

a machete and a huge cistern.

He grabbed the cistern and machete and approached the hive.

In one swift move, he cut the hive in two pieces, and inside that hive…was the biggest honey-comb that I ever saw.

All told, he collected over 45 pounds of the purest honey ever. Pure, dark gold Sicilian honey.

After we cleaned the place up and stowed the gear, the guy who owned the tomato farm next door stopped by in his truck.

"Saro," he said. "Be careful today. There is an enormous swarm of wasps that have attacked the local farmers. They are out of control. They are wasps, not bees. They are killing all the bees that we use to pollinate the melons. Everyone is looking for them"

Saro popped open the trunk. He took a handful of the honey and put it in his mouth.

"Not anymore" he said.

Now, every time I eat honey, I think of this story. Crispy critters and all. I love that guy. I truly do. Still, I can't believe what I saw that day. Truly remarkable.

Rachael Ray has a television program called "Europe on Forty Dollars a Day" where she visits European cities and attempts to feed herself on forty dollars for the entire day.

Forty dollars equates to roughly thirty euro a day, so I decided to give it a try for a week while in Sicily.

I would be the Sicilian version of Rachael Ray (her mom is Sicilian, by the way) and attempt to replicate her feat. Can it be done I thought?

First off, let me say that I am not considered cheap or frugal.

Lord knows that over my lifetime I have frittered away a king's ransom or two.

Truth be told, once my kids were grown up and settled a bit, I adopted the philosophy that not only will I be completely broke when I die, but the check to the undertaker will bounce.

If I have it, I decided, I will spend it. If I don't, then Uncle Sam will.

Thus, living on thirty euro a day would be a test for me. That's roughly forty dollars.

Like Rachael did, I will not count actual living expenses (rent, utilities, gas for the car, ect.). That will be the subject for another story.

No, I thought that I could live on an amount much cheaper than that, and I would test myself. After all, thirty euro a day means two hundred and ten euro a week, or roughly three hundred dollars.

If I food shopped at the grocery store I could easily beat Rachael. I know that because I usually spend less than eighty euro a week food shopping…but then I have to prepare the food.

This test would be just like hers, I thought. I will purchase things just like she does…already prepared.

That meant that I was going out to eat out every day for three meals, something I never do. I decided that I would be a tourist like Rachael and pretend that I didn't have a kitchen and that I was in a hotel somewhere.

I would calculate, just like Rachael did, actually eating three meals out every day, and try to fit a snack or two in between.

A. *Breakfast*

I eat light for breakfast every day…just like the Sicilians… so a cup of espresso and a brioche or a cup of espresso and a cornetto , which costs two euro and fifty cents, does the budget just fine.

Alternating my breakfast a bit, and switching to a cappuccino every other day, and also substituting other delicious breakfast rolls, I can have seven "breakfasts" a week for roughly twenty one euro total, or thirty dollars. If I want to include a nice glass of freshly squeezed orange juice (two euro a glass), that amount increases to four euro and fifty cents a day or five dollars and eighty five cents a day.

Round it off to six dollars a day for breakfast including the orange juice.

That leaves thirty four dollars a day for lunch and dinner and a snack.

B. *Lunch*

For lunch, I can have my choice of two slices of pizza (each cost two euro), or an arancini, which is a delicious rice ball for about two euro, or a slice of *scacciata* (meat pie, spinach pie, broccoli pie) for three euro or *pasta al forno* or *lasagna* (four euro) or any type of *panini* sandwich (four euro). A glass of wine is about two euro, or a soda (the same), and calculating the most expensive items just mentioned, that comes to six euro… seven dollars…give or take.

Thus with breakfast (six dollars) and lunch (seven dollars)…that still leaves twenty-seven dollars a day for snacks and dinner.

So far, it seems that I am right on schedule.

C. *Mid-Afternoon Snack*

Mid-afternoon, I can treat myself to a gelato (three euro), a granita (two euro), a cannoli (two euro), or any other Sicilian pastry (same price) plus a cappuccino or espresso.

Total cost for a mid-afternoon snack: five euro or seven dollars if you throw in a tip.

So far I have spent six dollars for breakfast, seven dollars for lunch, and seven dollars for a snack for a total of twenty dollars. I still have twenty dollars for a nice dinner.

D. *Dinner*

The average price for a good entrée at a decent *trattoria…scampi, vongole , stucco, cozze,* swordfish, any meat-based pasta, grilled meat assortment, grilled prawns, a whole pizza, a huge antipasto salad…is about twelve euro, including a half carafe of "vino di casa."

Throw in an after dinner aperitif, and round it off to fifteen euro… about nineteen dollars and fifty cents.

Let's see: six dollars for breakfast, seven dollars for lunch, seven dollars for a snack and twenty dollars for dinner. Forty dollars…or thirty euro…a day.

Did it!

If I want to still have money in my pocket, I'd eliminate the afternoon snack, the after dinner aperitif, or better still, go to a cheaper place for dinner where for twelve euro you can eat a "set" menu for under fifteen dollars.

See? It can be done.

Plus, I don't have a single dish to wash.

Seriously, I never eat out that much…nor do I eat that heavy. I usually eliminate the lunch and substitute dinner at that time, and during the evening eat a piece of fruit or a salad.

I bet if I sharpen my pencil a bit, I could save ten dollars more.

But why?

We are in Sicily, after all!

On the other hand, if you want to eliminate a lot of the carbs, cholesterol, and fat grams, you can stick to a fruit plate (about seven euro), or a nice salad (about five euro), and go from there.

Remember, if you are counting calories, then Sicily…with its fish, chicken, wide assortment of fresh veggies and fruit will be heaven for you!

Either way…as mom used to tell me…*Mangia*!

Living on a Bunch of Dimes

My earlier piece was on living in Sicily on forty dollars a day.

What if you scrimped and saved your money and wanted to splurge? How much does the typical "splurge" cost?

You can really light up the town if you wanted to go first class all the way.

Some of Europe's best chefs work at some of Sicily's finest restaurants, so if a person has it in his mind to be opulent and extravagant, this can be easily accomplished in Sicily. There is a whole set of rich, super rich, nouveau rich, and just plain filthy rich who visit Sicily regularly and have their own way of enjoying the Island.

Famous actors, actresses, writers, politicians, titans of industry world wide...all visit Sicily regularly.

I am not talking that kind of splurge. That would be a "dream" splurge...something that I could not experience. No, I am just talking about a "regular" splurge...by definition that is when you burst into tears at the end of the month when the credit card bill comes in and you realize that you are an idiot.

Here is a fantasy story for you that is true:

The names have been changed to protect the innocent.

This guy I know who is a lawyer (hmmm...sounds familiar already) hit a big case in America once and decided to live it large for a couple weeks in Sicily with his friends.

Living large was no problem for this guy.

It was the bane of his existence, as a matter of fact.

Selecting the nicest five-star hotel that he could find, he found a hotel at the foot of Taormina...on the beach.

This section of Taormina is called "Taormina Mare"...home of a string of five-star hotels frequented by the world's jet setters.

Since he really wasn't a jet setter, rather a guy who had a few bucks that were absolutely burning a hole in his pocket, he figured "what the heck" and decided to splurge this one time.

He had visited the hotel before...as a guest of his friend...and made a promise to himself that someday...just once...he would stop taking economy tours and would live large.

The hotel was owned by an old and venerable Austrian family who later sold it to a small chain of luxury hotel owners.

They had poured millions of euro re-furbishing the place and as a result the hotel rapidly picked up the reputation as THE destination in Sicily.

All these rich people and me...err...my friend.

The first thing he learned at that first dinner was that he had to immediately go out the next day and buy decent clothing.

Everyone had either a tuxedo or a Gucci suit on, and the women were dripping in jewels.

We decided (I mean he decided) to eat in his room that first night and prepare for their "grand entrance" the next night.

Getting up early the next morning, he and his friend high-tailed it to the clothing shops.

Three thousand dollars later, they were prepared...barely prepared... but hey, what the heck.

That evening, they dressed to the nines.

He made a dashing figure, even if I do say so myself. She was ok too.

Getting off the elevator, dapper in his new duds and she in her evening attire, they made their grand entrance.

However, that night was "Hawaiian" night.

Dress down night. Geez.

He thought he was in Honolulu.

Everyone was in Hawaiian garb. Complete with leis.

For the second night, we, I mean he, ate in.

He found out that for the week every night was a "theme" night: Hawaiian one night, Algerian another, German another, and so on.

Seems a party of Europeans had flown in and had taken over the place. Oh well.

Here he was, in a place that cost 500 euro a night...and he had to buy a complete wardrobe for dinner every night that he would never use again.

To make a long story short, the next day they both returned the fancy duds they had purchased for that first grand entrance (thank God), and spent the next two days on the beach gawking at "le nouveau riche"

At night, they avoided the dinner parties.

My friend still had a great time though.

They just ate pizza at the local pizzeria.

And saved a bundle.

They checked-out a week later, satisfied that rubbing elbows with the elite wasn't all that it was cracked out to be.

He realized that money wasn't a pre-requisite to enjoying himself in Sicily. Quite the opposite. Visiting Sicily is what a particular visitor wants to make of it, I decided that the "old" way of visiting Sicily...my regular way...was best for me.

Still, I loved that hotel...I mean, he loved that hotel!

About ten months ago, American tenants that I had rented my condo to, trashed it.

I had rented it to them for a week, and they pretty much destroyed my place.

After they left, Massimo called me and informed me that things were broken, things were missing and trash was everywhere.

"That's it," I thought to myself. "No more, I am done renting my place out."

A year previously, another couple had broken a brand new sofa that I was still paying off, and this call from Massimo was the last straw.

Massimo suggested that I try to find local Sicilians who could take care of the place while I was in America and help defray the monthly expenses.

Since the economy was going bad in America and I was watching my pennies, I thought that was a good idea.

But who?

I needed someone that I could trust and ask for advice.

Sicilian beaches are among the world's finest!

I didn't want to create a bigger problem than I already had, as the Italian eviction laws are profoundly slow...sometimes taking years...and I didn't want any part of that.

I called my friend Maria Pace and asked her for advice.

"Alfred" she said, "I think I know someone."

About an hour later, she called back.

"Alfred" she said, "We are in luck. One of Alessio's friends is looking for a place with his girlfriend"

Alessio was Maria's very handsome boyfriend.

He is a doctor in Catania (a radiologist) and his friend owned a business in my ancestral hometown of Trecastagni.

"Perfetto" I said. "I want to meet them."

That evening Maria and Alessio came by the place with their two friends Alessandro and Antonia.

Since Alessandro was from Trecastagni, he already had a large chit in his favor. Antonia was also my mom's name, so I was beginning to feel that the stars were beginning to align themselves.

The five of us sat on the deck and had a drink.

Maria explained to me that the both of them needed a place to live for about a year, as they were saving their money to buy a house.

Antonia reminded me of my daughters. *Petit*, quiet, beautiful. I found out that she was from Palermo.

Alessandro was handsome. He was tall, intelligent, and most importantly, appeared serious about his life.

They were just what I was looking for.

We quickly struck a deal. They would pay rent to me, plus a chunk of all the utilities.

They asked if they could move some of their personal possessions including furniture into the place, and I didn't mind.

Over the next six months, Antonia transformed my condo into a real Sicilian "home."

On the front foyer and the rear deck she placed many flower pots. She planted all sorts of herbs. She scrubbed the place from top to bottom.

As I got to know them, as time went on, I first grew to respect them. Then to love them.

They are part of the "new breed" of Sicilian youngsters.

Serious. Dedicated. Responsible.

I just love it.

When I arrived on Christmas Day this year, I arrived at the condo to find it aglow in Christmas decorations and warmth.

Antonia was busy in the kitchen cooking supper. She is a real catch I thought, and I hope Alessandro realizes that they broke the mold when they made her.

She not only cooks, keeps herself in shape by going to the gym every day, she is well read, articulate, bottles her own preserves, has a green thumb, cooks like a gourmet chef, and is generally a one of a kind gal.

I also realized that the dream of home ownership is rapidly escaping these young kids as housing keep skyrocketing in Sicily while jobs keep disappearing.

Looking at her, I realized that this generation of Sicilian youngsters might be the last generation of Sicilians that are truly 'Sicilian."

This upset me a lot.

However, I realized again just how resourceful Sicilians have been over the centuries, and it dawned on me that I was actually HELPING them by offering a place to rent for a while while they saved their money to buy their own place.

Like true Sicilians…and thanks to Maria Pace…we had found each other.

Looking back at it now, I am glad those Americans trashed the condo.

I think I came out way ahead.

My favorite view...from my deck in Aci Catena.

Gadgets

In Sicily, I can't wait until things get dirty.

I just love using my washing machine.

I have one of those European models…that doesn't have that center agitator that American models have.

It tumbles the clothes clean, fresh and just wonderful. It is truly a remarkable washing machine.

While I have the best washing machine ever, I do not have a clothes dryer. Huh? Clothes dryer in Sicily? The *Isola del sole?* The Island of the Sun?

No one has a clothes dryer in Sicily.

Instead, I have one of those plastic things that unfolds on the deck where I put the clothes on it to dry.

What a combination. A great machine and Mother Nature.

Another thing I love is my toaster.

Here, the toasters don't "pop" when the toast is done.

You slip the toast into these metal compartments and wait over the toaster for the bread to toast.. It doesn't pop.

My mom had one just like this…back in the 1950s.

If you leave the toast in too long, it will burn.

This is ok with me.

I remember when I was a little kid, my mom burned the toast all the time. She was always so busy chasing me, my brother, or my sister around that she would remember the toaster only after the room was filled with smoke.

For years, I thought the routine one used to make toast was to toast it until it was black, then scrape the blackened toast off with a knife.

That's how my mom did it.

She burned the toast every single morning. However, she made it with love.

Thus, when I bought this toaster, I was very happy. It was a throw-back toaster.

Just like home.

Toast the bread, scrape it, and then eat it.

Heaven.

Another gadget I love here is the ice cube tray.

Visualize a ten cents piece…a dime. Something about one half of an inch in diameter.

That's how big the ice cubes are. No bigger than half an inch.

You need about fifteen to get anything cold. Remarkable.

Finally, the trash can in the house.

There is none.

Everyone puts their trash in plastic bags from the grocery store and then throws them away every day.

Sounds inconvenient, but you have never met Sicilian ants, have you?

If ANYTHING is left out overnight, forget it. They will cart it and you away!

This year, the Italian Government passed a new re-cycling law. Plastic trash bags are now outlawed. Now, plastic, paper, and waste have to separated.

Sicilians are going crazy over this.

However, 28% of all of Europe's trash is created by Italians and almost all landfills are filled to capacity.

In Naples, trash everywhere is now commonplace.

Another interesting thing is the "bidet' in the bathrooms. I find it interesting how indispensable European women find these things, yet most American women, when they see one for the first time say "Oh, so THAT'S a bidet…how do you use it?"

Like I would know.

I have one in each bathroom, as does each house in Sicily and Italy. They are indispensable, I am told.

Kitchen utensils are another interesting set of gadgets in Sicily. I find particularly useful a certain type of pan …actually it is a *fish grilling pan*… that everyone uses when they grill fish on the stove. The pan has ridges on it…like a waffle iron…and to use it properly; a thin coat of olive oil is brushed on these ridges and the put on the stove. When the pan is HOT, the fish is put on.

The secret is the marinade on the fish which is prepared first: a simple mixture of lemon juice, olive oil, and fresh chopped parsley. The fish is

My dad, Santo "Sonny" Zappala, and my mom Antoinette "Toni" Zappala. I ate many a scraped piece of toast during my childhood! I am the little one in the middle.

brushed on both sides and put in the pan.

The rest of the marinade is put on the fish AFTER it is cooked. Once you eat fish this way, you will never bake a fish again, believe me.

Dishware itself is interesting…and is probably the reason that Sicilians are not as big as Americans. Dinner plates, pasta plates, soup plates are all a bit smaller than our plates. Thus, serving sizes are smaller. Pasta, for example, is served in 100 gram portions…enough to fill a Sicilian pasta plate…but roughly half the size of a normal "American" portion.

Still, no one seems to complain, and second helpings of pasta are rare.

Washing machines, toasters, trash receptacles, ice cube trays, bidets, fish grilling pans, dinnerware…plus a million other gadgets…make Sicily a fun place to live.

Even if you have to scrape the toast!

"Capodanno" is New Year's Eve in Italy.

Like Americans, Sicilians either stay home and celebrate privately or in small groups, or go to fancy restaurants for planned events, or visit friends for a New Year's party.

A few years ago, I enjoyed myself immensely in Taormina at a wonderful restaurant there.

This year, however, was a completely new experience.

I attended a New Year's party at the home of one Trecastagni's most prominent families at the invitation of my friends Alessandro and Alessio, the boyfriends of Maria Pace and Antonia , my now adopted Sicilian daughters.

Both Alessandro and Alessio had gone to school with two of the brothers who owned this house and the invitation was extended to me to join them.

I wanted to attend this party for two reasons: first, the name of the street that the party was to be held was Via Zappalà (my last name) and second, by attending a New Year's party in Trecastagni it would be the first time in over a century (since both my grandfathers emigrated to America), that someone from my family would welcome in the New Year there.

Thus, I had a hidden agenda for accepting the invitation.

I knew this wouldn't be a casual affair, and was thankful that I had a nice sports jacket and slacks to wear. Tonight I wasn't under dressed as I normally am.

"Casual-elegant" would describe the garb that everyone wore this particular evening.

Arriving at the party at 10 PM (in Sicily, nothing starts before 10 PM, believe me), I had followed my friends in my car so that if I tired early I could slip out and not disrupt my friend's evening.

I knew the way up the mountain to Trecastagni very well as I had traveled up and down this road hundreds of times over the years.

Proceeding past the center of Trecastagni and actually on the way out of town and heading further up the mountain, we found the house...or should I say mansion.

The house was enormous. Bigger than enormous. Perhaps one of the biggest, if not the biggest houses in the area.

As I later found out, the lower level of the house where the party was to be held was the first level of the house.

There were two other levels. Believe me when I say this: each "level" of this house would swallow up the average American house. Each level went literally on and on it seemed.

Walking into this architectural wonder, we were greeted by two of the brothers, Maximilian and Alessandro (yes, another Alessandro…Sicily's most popular name for men the last twenty years).

I was introduced to the girlfriend of Maximilian, a wonderful German woman of about thirty-three years who made Sicily her home. She spoke perfect English, although she had a slight Irish tinge to it. I later found out that she had worked for six years in Ireland and now was working for a big company in Sicily. She was completely fluent in Italian, English and German, and I was impressed.

The other girlfriend was another remarkable woman. She acted as the hostess of the party, and judging from her demeanor, was in charge of setting things up.

The first room that we entered, on the ground floor was an open concept *cucina*…a kitchen as big as any restaurant's that I have seen. On the right was an enormous wood-fired pizza oven. On the left, state of the art appliances. The kitchen was commercial grade and huge.

The kitchen area opened into an enormous dining area that had been set up with a twenty -foot table, already loaded with just about anything edible that could be found in Sicily.

I couldn't take my eyes off that table to tell you the truth.

Resisting the urge to just dive on the table, I continued on with the obligatory house tour.

The dining area opened to a large sitting area/ fireplace room. Interestingly enough…this room had knotty-pine wood on its walls…highly unusual for Sicily.

A roaring fireplace was already going…later they would barbecue the *salsiccia* on the hearth…but for now, the ambiance was astounding.

The walls of this room were covered with rare and expensive original works of art; on one antique table were treasures from Africa, Europe, Asia…the kind of things you would see on the television program "Antique Road Show." The book shelves were lined with complete works of art books from just about every famous European artist.

Other shelving has works from the great Italian writers.

Singularly, this room took my breath away. The epitome of elegance. I thought to myself that I would love to spend an evening here with perhaps a cognac in hand looking through this astounding book collection.

This room then opened into the dance area.

The dance area room contained a working bar, a dance floor, sitting tables, and an array of electronic equipment that rivaled Taormina's finest discos. State of the art electronics. Flat Screen TVs were mounted on the walls, and tucked into one corner…a collection of antique musical instruments that would make any collector drool.

Frankly, I never had seen such a wonderful collection of art in a home.

For the next hour, I wandered the rooms, gawking at the various collections, my attention disrupted only by the greetings offered by the arriving guests.

To me, the party and food was be the "extra" this evening.

By 11 PM, the thirty or so guests had all arrived as this party was to be a small intimate affair.

I was a little nervous about the fog which had begun to roll in as I made the drive up the mountain, so I decided that it would be prudent to drink only non-alcoholic beverages this night.

Those cork-screw roads up the mountain would challenge any driver, and I had no intention of driving with any alcohol in me.

My fears were later confirmed when I drove home as I fought to see even two inches in front of me. The fog on the way home later was simply treacherous. The decision not to drink was a good one.

Thank God I had made that decision.

Now, however, it was time to eat.

And eat we did.

Think about any and every conceivable Sicilian dish that you know… it was on that table that night.

I tried the "scacciata" that Alessandro's mom made, the eggplant parmigiana that Maria made, some "involtini di carne" (rolled and grilled meat), and of course the *salsiccia*. I had micro-servings of each; I wanted to leave room for everything.

The local cheeses, olives, salami, parma, peppers, vegetables, rice dishes, penne pasta dishes, were other things that I sampled in small portions.

Believe me, it was a challenge not to over-eat that night, but I did fairly well considering all the temptations.

Of course, lentils were served. "I lenticchi"...Sicilians eat a bowl of lentils at midnight, as the belief is that since they are small, like money, it is good luck to eat them at midnight. Luck will follow, they say.

At the stroke of midnight, the champagne began to flow, and thus started my favorite time of the night...next to eating everything in sight, that is...kissing all the pretty women on both cheeks while saying either "Auguri! "or "Buon Anno!"

Then the dancing began. Lots of it.

Strangely, all the tunes were American.

Saturday Night Fever is still popular here after all these years, as is that song YMCA (God, I hate that tune), Brittany Spears, Michael Jackson, and all the popular tunes that we hear in America.

After watching the Sicilians attempt to imitate "Dancing With The Stars" on the dance floor, I concluded that American men and women are better dancers than Sicilians, and to prove the point, I tripped the light fantastic a time or two myself.

After a sufficient amount of time of strutting my stuff, and still fearful of the ride home, I said my good byes and departed.

By this time, however, the fog had gotten twenty times worse.

I traveled one mile per hour thru the fog bank, my heart in my mouth. My hands clutched the driving wheel as I struggled to find my way. Remember...this was a cork-screw mountain road!

However, due to my superior American driving skills, I managed to crawl down the hill. Really, I have no driving skills. I made it due to the grace of God and the fact that a big truck got in front of me and it had fog lights. I was saved!

I made it.

My grandfather Alfio M. Zappala, my father Santo, and my grandmother Agostina "Zina' Lascola Zappala. I was happy to ring in the New Year in Trecastagni because I was the first of my clan to do so since Alfio came to America in the early 20th century. Interestingly enough, Alfio did not know my other grandfather Gaetano Torrisi in Trecastagni, but the two became fast friends in America.

Arriving at home at 3 AM, I decided to wait up for Antonia and Alessandro who arrived at 5 AM, looking pretty worn out themselves.

Sleeping until noon the next day, I wondered what new adventure I would enjoy.

"Alfred" I thought "You have set the bar pretty high. Here's hoping that you can have as much fun today"

Geez, for an old guy, I seem to keep entertaining myself pretty well!

And best of all, I keep meeting new and wonderful people. And better than that, a wonderful experience on yet another wonderful New Year's Eve is now tucked away in my mind!

There are a million history books on Sicily out there...some good, some not so good, some bad.

While I have no intention of giving you a history lesson or turn this book into a history book, there are certain names throughout history that maybe you should be familiar with.

I do think, however, that you should have a "working knowledge" of at least a few of the more interesting characters and groups from both Sicily's distant past and the immediate past. Thus, I have chosen to tell you about a few of them that maybe will motivate you to do additional research on your own.

Of the thousands of characters who have helped make Sicily what it is today, some of these people helped shape Sicily, some exploited Sicily, or some had no influence on it whatsoever.

Hopefully, my thumb-nail description of some of these people/groups will peek your curiosity and cause you to Google a few of them.

A. The Way Back Machine: Gelone (or Gelo)

Let's get in the WAY BACK MACHINE and travel back in time.

Back to a time when Western civilization tottered on the brink of extinction. Back to a time when a tiny group of Greeks, Spartans to be exact, held off the invading Persian Empire lead by Xerxes in Greece.

We all studied about Leonardis and the 300 Spartans, and how they held back a 300,000 strong invading Persian army for three days at Thermopylae while the rest of Greece gathered its reinforcements.

As the story goes, the Athenians and the Spartans later defeated the Persians thanks to Leonardis' sacrifice with his band of 300, but is that really the whole story?

Well, no.

Back in Sicily, the Greeks who had long settled in Sicily were waging their own battle against allies of the Persians: The Carthaginians, the Phoenicians, and even other Greeks who had sold out to the Persians.

Had this invading group of Carthaginians and Phoenicians been successful in Sicily, their forces would have later re-enforced Xerxes' forces and probably would have tipped the outcome of the "Battle for Western Civilization" in their favor.

History, as they say, would have been re-written. Had Xerxes been successful in Greece, democracy would have never been born there…and who knows what life would be like today.

One guy prevented this from happening in Sicily. One guy defeated the invading hordes: Gelo (The Italian pronunciation) or Gelone (The English pronunciation).

Either way, this guy was one tough cookie.

He is known in history as "The Tyrant of Siracusa."

Really, Siracusa (and many other Sicilian cities for that matter) had many "tyrants" during this time period, because the basic definition of a "tyrant" is "one who takes over by force" according to the dictionary. Thus, if you were a brute, and had an army to back you up, you ended up as a tyrant somewhere.

Since French wasn't yet invented and the term "coup d'état" wasn't yet coined, he (and the others) have been stuck with this term.

Thus, the tyrant Gelone…perhaps had a hand in saving what is now Western culture.

Was he cruel? Definitely. Did he exploit the Siracusian people? Absolutely.

However, when it came time to step to the plate and defend Sicily, his forces inflicted hundreds of thousands of casualties on the invaders and tremendously weakened this threat to Sicily (and the West) for decades afterwards.

Not that he loved the Greeks that much either.

When the Greeks later asked him to send troops to Greece to help them against Xerxes, he said that he would be happy to do this provided that they name him as commander in chief of all Greek forces.

The Greeks refused, and he contented himself with wiping out the remainng enemy in Sicily while the battle raged in Greece.

However, had the two enemy forces linked up, that is the forces of Persia and the forces of Carthage linked up, the result would have been a different world today.

Gelone is someone who is definitely worth researching a bit more, as this time period is a very interesting time period in Sicily's past.

B. *The Romans*

Here's the thing about the Roman occupation of Sicily: they did Sicilians no favors.

Back in the third century BC was when the "fun" started. The problem was that the tyrants of Syracuse backed the wrong horse in a huge war, and as a result Sicily was lost to Rome.

The Siracusans chose to back Carthage in its war against Rome in the Second Punic War.

Bad move. Politics at its worst. This should have never happened, but greed does strange things to many people, it seems.

You remember this war: The famous general Hannibal from Carthage...after causing havoc all over the Roman Empire and defeating Roman army after Roman army, crossed the Alps with his army (including his elephants) and actually hurled his spear over the gates of Rome...before finally being force to retreat.

Not only was he forced to retreat, he was forced to accept terrible peace terms with Rome which ultimately Carthage couldn't accept, and Rome later annihilated Carthage, destroying the city and as legend has it...not leaving two stones on top of each other there.

As you can see, the Romans were not in a happy mood with the Greeks from Siracusa who were running things in Sicily.

As they say, payback was swift.

Retribution complete.

By 210 BC, Rome had conquered all of Sicily, enslaving the population, murdering those who had supported Carthage, and generally making Sicily into a colony of Rome.

Sicilians were not granted citizenship as Romans, by the way, for nearly five hundred years afterwards...and only because by then...the third century AD... Rome itself falling apart and it was purely a desperation move to keep the Roman Empire together.

During those five centuries, as occupiers usually do, the Romans did things to benefit *themselves* first and foremost... in this case they exploited the agricultural capabilities of Sicily unwisely.

Sicily became Rome's bread basket.

Her wheat fed Rome.

Sicily also became Rome's source for lumber too.

Forests (yes, there were once forests in Sicily…streams and rivers too!) were cut down, put on boats and sent to Rome during those five centuries.

Over time, Romans eventually succumbed to Sicily's charms and built wonderful summer villas, beautiful amphitheaters, and Roman baths… again to benefit them, not the Sicilians.

Today, Sicily is awash with many of these ruins.

Cicero spent time here. So did Cato. So did many famous Romans. For five hundred years, Romans injected the Roman Way on Sicily.

And cross-pollinated the population too.

One of my favorite of the hundreds of testimonies to Roman occupation still in existence today for all to see, study, and enjoy is located in Casale, outside of the town of Piazza Armerina. There, the ruins of a forty room Roman villa once owned by an obviously wealthy Roman… and perfectly preserved from time…are studied and visited by thousands every year. The mosaic work alone is worth the trip to this site. It is really a wonderful testimony to this time period.

The amphitheater in Taormina, still used today by famous singers every summer as they give their concerts, was refurbished by the Romans and Catania also has wonderful ruins too of this era. Many areas of Sicily were touched by the Romans…and deep down Sicilians are proud of this link to Rome's glorious past. However, if you were a Sicilian living during this time period, you wouldn't be too happy.

One quick story before I end this part. Remember Cleopatra, the Egyptian ruler who was smuggled into the room of Julius Caesar in a rolled up rug and seduced him? Well, it was a Sicilian fisherman who smuggled her in!

Like all the occupiers, if you balance what the Romans took versus what they left behind, in my view, the scale is tipped always against the Sicilian people.

C. *The Saracens*

Honestly, if one more person tells me that the Saracens made advances for the Sicilian people during their occupation of Sicily in agriculture, science, mathematics, or that they invented the *cannoli, granita,* brought olives and oranges to Sicily, built road and buildings there, or any of the other ten thousand things that I have read about that they did while the occupied Sicily from the middle of the ninth century until they were finally kicked out by the Normans in the eleventh century, I think I am going to scream.

What these people who rave about Saracen contribution always seem to forget is that did all those things for themselves, and no one else.

As for the Sicilians?

They were ruled by the boot…and the sword.

They were enslaved by the hundreds of thousands…for damn near three hundred years.

Whole populations were sometimes wiped out. For example, in Taormina, every inhabitant there was slaughtered when the Sarcens conquered it.

I have no use for the Saracens. None.

As harsh as that sounds, I guess I really feel that way.

Besides massacring Sicilians, tens of thousands more were sent to North Africa and enslaved…especially Sicilian women.

All in the name of religion.

This was the era of Muslim conquest.

And conquer they did…approaching almost the very gates of Rome before they were repelled.

I bet if you asked any of those Sicilians who were massacred or enslaved if they wanted to eat a cannoli or be enslaved, you'd know the answer.

Saracens…collectively Moors, Arabs, Berbers, and people from either Africa or the Middle East were themselves overwhelmed in the decades before by zealous believers of Islam.

This was the period of religious zeal and fervor. Convert or be enslaved.

The Christian cult reacted slowly to this threat and as a result, organized resistance in Sicily, Spain and parts of Europe was not cohesive or coordinated…because the Europeans themselves were too busy killing themselves and competing for power.

What a terrible time it was for sure.

Death and destruction was everywhere.

When the last fortified town in Sicily fell, Taormina, not only was the Catholic bishop there killed, but his heart was cut out while still beating and eaten by the Saracen commander…in front of the citizens of Taormina…who themselves were all killed.

Nice, huh?

During the occupation, non-Muslims had to stand up every time a Muslim entered a room, could not ring church bells, could not own a weapon, they had to wear identification markings on their clothing, they had to pay heavy taxes, they could not built churches, they could not have religious processions, they could read the Bible so that a Muslim could hear them, they could not drink wine, they could not ride horses, they could not put a saddle on their mules, they could not bear arms, plus, they could not marry a Muslim woman.

Not exactly tolerant, were they?

Sounds to me like they were a thousand times worse than Bin Laden ever was, to tell you the truth.

Fortunately, after three centuries of oppression, the Normans came and gave them a dose of their own medicine, driving each and every one of them out of Sicily in a reverse blood bath as they reclaimed Sicily for Christianity.

Nope, the Saracens did not come in peace. Most left feet first, thankfully.

Like the Romans, anything and everything they did was self serving.

They raped Sicily and her people and that's the truth.

Of course, what they did was rivaled only by the Spanish, who arrived a few centuries later.

Not that I am an expert by any means, but on the other hand, I know oppression when I see it.

As for me? My last name is Zappalà. Arabic from "Za Allah." This means "from Allah."

I think I have a Saracen gene or two floating around from this period of time.

Wow!

D. *The Norman Era*

I love these guys.

Despite being around only for a short period of time, they got a tremendous amount accomplished while they were in Sicily. Light shined on Sicily for a while under their rule. A good light.

I bet you are familiar with this period of time.

It was the Eleventh Century and the Moors and Arabs were threatening to conquer everybody and install their way of life on all of Europe.

Most of Spain was under Muslim domination already.

However, like today, some Muslims just can't seem to get along with one another.

Within the Muslim religion, fundamental religious difference just cannot be reconciled, and add in the plunder and power that comes from conquering a foreign land, in no time flat comes the bickering for power and political intrigue...just like today.

They began to lose battles as the Europeans slowly got their act together.

The pope back then finally got around to getting his head unstuck from the sand and began to ask different European groups to defend Christianity and organize armies in its defense.

It was within these tumultuous times that the Normans were asked by the pope to lead an expedition and help free Sicily from domination... and included as additional help here for the Normans were some of the Saracens themselves.

Political intrigue, remember.

In any case, for over a hundred year period starting in the second half of the eleventh century, thanks to a small Christian army led by Robert "The Guiscard" and his brother Roger I of Hauteville who initially freed Sicily from Saracen domination, the Normans ruled.

This dynasty gave also two of perhaps the most enlightened of Sicily's rulers: William I and William II.

Palermo was turned into Europe's cultural center during this period.

Great men in science, mathematics, and the arts gathered in the king's court. The hundreds of mosques in Palermo were converted into churches.

Spectacular things happened during the period of awakening.

When the dynasty ended a mere 100 years later and control transferred to another dynasty, the Hohenstaufen's Dynasty, another wonder briefly blessed Sicily: the reign of the great Frederick II, known as "Stupor

Mundi"...the Wonder of the World.

During his reign, Palermo hit its zenith...as the intellectual, scientific and literary masters from all Europe were present in his court. Palermo was the shining city of Europe, and did she prosper.

After his death however, things were never the same. Sicily slowly backslid and again became a bit player in Europe's history, but for a brief time, the Normans had truly created Sicily's golden age.

Make no mistake about it: Had the Normans not driven out the Saracens, none of this would have happened.

Today, The Norman influence is still in full view for all to see.

I see it every day as I take my daily walk in Aci Castello, home to the Norman Castle...in all its glory...and in many towns from Catania, Taormina, Cefalù and of course Palermo still feel its influence.

This era is a fascinating era to research and learn about, and many scholars have written wonderful books on the era.

Of all, this era is my personal favorite.

E. *The Spanish*

I am not a fan of the five hundred year domination of Sicily by the Spanish.

Not at all.

During this five hundred year period, which ended around the time of the American Civil War, Europe was a mess. Spain, France, England, Austria, all took turns fighting for power.

Millions died in war, plague and hunger haunted Europe.

For a period of time, Spain controlled the New World, and also had vast holdings in Europe and elsewhere. Sicily was swallowed up in this five century Spanish abyss.

It didn't have a chance.

It missed much of what was going on in the rest of Europe as a result. It was too busy getting its people dragged back to serfdom, or seeing them killed or having its natural raw materials wiped out by the Spanish.

By the time the ruling Bourbons were kicked out, nary a tree existed.

Or a stream or river.

The wealthy "barons" sucked everything away, often on the backs of the people.

Starting with the Middle Age, moving on to the Renaissance, the Enlightenment, and all the major eras that helped shape European thought, with the Spanish occupation, things in Sicily froze in time.

Sicily was a political pawn. Swapped like a trading card.

Exploited by the "barons" of Spain…wealthy land owners turned Sicily back into feudal times…and ultimately led to the start of the great exodus of Sicilians out of Sicily by the late nineteenth century.

To understand what Spain was doing during this era, all you have to do is to see what Spain was doing to Central and South America back then.

Killing lots of people in the name of Christ.

Ask the Incas. Ask the Aztecs.

There, they subjugated the people. Hauling the treasures of Central and South America back to Spain.

Imperialism at its abject worst.

Sicily returned to the Middle Ages again, and seemed to be stuck there. Poverty was the rule, not the exception under Spanish rule.

During this time, the "good" mafia was formed…initially to fight against this ruthless oppression, but only to be quickly co-opted into the "bad" mafia…changing over time to paid thugs who enforced the wishes of the wealthy landowners by exploiting high rents and taxes from the tenant farmers.

In short, it was a dark period in her history.

To make matters worse, many natural disasters struck during this period to further push Sicily back into the abyss.

An eruption of Etna destroyed completely Catania in 1669 followed by a series of devastating earthquakes that wiped out 5% of the entire population.

Surrounded by rampant disease, oppression, exploitation, and thuggery…would you want to live there?

The whole thing ended. (Really? Did it end or has nothing changed? That question is still being debated) when Garibaldi and his band of 1000, aided by the Sicilian peasants who took up arms on his behalf defeated the Bourbon army in the Battle of Calatafimi on May 15, 1860.

By July of that year, the Bourbon regime was in retreat, and in a "vote" by the people several months later, a stunning 99% of the voters decided to unify with Italy and Garibaldi handed Sicily to the House of Savoy.

The above paragraph is subject to multiple interpretations. Some believe the vote was rigged: peasants couldn't vote.

Others believe that nothing changed under the Savoy Regime.

I agree with the last part.

By the turn of the century, hundreds of thousands of Sicilians were leaving for America, Australia, and South America for a better life.

Then the First World War broke out killing many more Sicilians.

Then the Fascists and Mussolini came, followed by the devastation of the Second World War, the rise of the mafia and….

Geez, it just didn't end, did it?

In any case, as I said above, I just am not a fan of the Spanish.

Now you can see why.

By the way, my grandfather Gaetano Torrisi...Torrisi is derived from the Spanish *Torressi*.

Guess I shouldn't complain too much, should I?

So, Exactly Who Wears the Pants in a Sicilian House?

I pondered this deep and moving question many times.

After observing hundreds of Sicilian family households, I think I am as qualified as any to render a judgment.

Here is the answer: The man is the head of the household. Only because the woman of the household lets him think that way.

In the final analysis, the women call the shots but the men think they do.

Brilliant.

Any moron knows the reason for this as well.

Clearly, the feminine gender is vastly superior to the male gender.

The genius, I found out, is to never let the male figure that out!

The man does almost nothing in a typical Sicilian household other than being the bread winner (although many women hold jobs outside of the house, the man still does basically nothing. The woman works twice as hard, that's all.)

This goes way back culturally, perhaps as far back as the Muslim occupation where women were fully veiled with the burka and closeted in the home.

As each subsequent group occupied Sicily, each culture slowly integrated their culture into the nuclear family and it evolved to what it is today.

Except the women have evolved more, I think.

Not to generalize too much here, but the women I know get their cooking skills passed down from their side of the family.

Then she augments those skills by learning from the husband's mother a few of his favorite things.

A mutated cuisine is thus created.

For example, a woman from Palermo who marries a man from Siracusa will initially feed him what he wants, but over time she will feed him what she wants but when he eats it, he thinks it is what he wants.

Superior genes win every time.

Usually, the man lays down the law with the kids, but mom is always the court of last resort...just like in America.

The Sicilian daughter returns home; mom and my daughter Jennifer the day that mom visited her ancestral home in Trecastagni. In the background is Saro Messina and Mr. Messina, the present owner of the family house. Mom told me later that this day was the happiest day of her life. That tree that you see was planted by her mom before she left for America over a century ago.

The modern Sicilian woman is now educated, with many holding college and professional degrees.

Thus, the feminine beast is that more equipped to dominate.

Geez.

To me, that's what I call "piling on."

Woman are loyal to their men too.

I haven't found many floozies here, despite my best efforts over the years. The floozies that I do see are usually transplants from some other European countries.

While there are exceptions, the vast majority of Sicilian women hold the highest moral values…as opposed to the men, who are…well, Sicilian men.

When men congregate together, a wolf pack mentality sometime takes over, and if a pretty woman passes by, the cat calls and whistles start. However, a lone wolf guy would never do that.

If a woman has children with her, even the wolf pack remains silent.

Thus, my observation concludes the following: As is the case in just about every spot in the world, women dominate their men and men are oblivious to that.

Sheer genius, that species.

Incredible, actually.

The Sicilian woman: God's perfect creation.

The Panettone

I will nibble on maybe one piece of *panettone* a year.

Usually, it is because I have to be polite.

Seriously, while the panettone is adored and glorified in Italy, in America is it just one other desert offering lost in the holiday array of offerings.

While is taste pleasant enough, my mouth doesn't exactly water when I think about eating one.

While it IS a part of the holiday festivities in my house, to me, it is not the centerpiece.

Here is a primer for you on the *panettone* just in case you want to experiment. The vocabulary can be tricky, so please pay attention.

Legend has it that this guy named Tony invented the *panettone*.

As I understand it, the king was coming to town for a visit and the local dignitaries forgot to order the sweets. They turned to Tony, who was a baker of bread and he invented the *panettone* by throwing in butter, raisins, and a few other things. When the king ate it, he loved it. Thus was created *Pane* (bread) by Tone (Tony): *Panettone*.

I don't believe that story for a minute. I think the guys from Milan and Verona, where millions are produced yearly, invented that story as a marketing tool.

And what a stroke of genius it was.

Nowadays, from November fifteenth until Christmas every store in Italy has a mountain of them piled high at every check out counter.

First are the cheap ones...they use margarine instead of butter.

For five euro or so, you can buy one of these for your office colleagues.

However, for the family get together, don't even think of this version. For family gatherings, the all butter variety is necessary...these can vary vastly in price from seven euro to twenty euro depending on the manufacturer.

Some manufacturers put *panettone* in the same boxes you see in America. Others put them in very fancy and elegant boxes. Other put them in colored tin foil and tie them with a beautiful ribbon.

Thus, the selection of a panettone requires a great deal of thought based on who the recipient will be.

The boss gets a good one. The mother in law gets the best one.

Just to be sure that the inventory is completely depleted by the end of the first week of January, clever marketers created "La Festa della Befana" where people give…*panettone*!

Talk about a final inventory depleater! What a stroke of genius again!

By that time, the prices have been reduced to a pittance at the markets and everyone usually gets the best ones which by now have been placed on sale.

The connoisseur of these delectable delights knows also about the many mutant versions…the *pandoro* for instance, which to me tastes like angel- food cake with a little confectionary sugar sprinkled on top.

Pandoro have no raisins, just the heavenly goodness that the manufacturer chooses to use ingredients-wise.

For the truly cultured and sophisticated, they have the *pandoro* stuffed with different creams, like pistachio cream, lemon cream, hazelnut cream, chocolate cream but the price for these delights can be high.

In Rome, I saw some for twenty five euro…of course, the packaging was superb. But still…thirty bucks for one of these? C'mon.

In any case, the panettone and pandoro are deeply ingrained in Italian society today.

I just do not understand why someone would reach for a slice of that stuff when the *cannoli* tray is right next to it.

Or the ricotta cake.

More for me, I guess.

When I was a kid, it was a mortal sin if you ate meat on Friday. That's what the nuns told me.

If you ate a hot dog on a Friday, you'd burn in hell, I was told.

Yikes.

That's a pretty steep price to pay for a hot dog or a ham sandwich, I always thought.

When The Second Vatican Council took place in the late 1960s, all of a sudden you could eat meat. You could also say the Mass in English, play folk tunes during Mass, could not pray in Latin, and Saint Christopher no longer was the saint of safe travel.

Everything changed. And I for one wasn't very fond of the changes. Tradition, it seemed, went out the window. Plus, what about all those Saint Christopher medals I had?

I often wondered about the guy who ate meat in the nineteen fifties and was condemned to hell.

Did he get out when the rules were changed? Or is he still there?

Imagine him meeting Saddam Hussein, Osama Bin Laden or Adolph Hitler in hell today.

The conversation would go something like this:

The guy: "What are you in for?"

Saddam: "I gassed three hundred thousand. You?"

The guy: "I ate a ham sandwich."

Hmm.

In any case, on Fridays we ate fish, eggs (although eggs are technically from a chicken and thus should have been covered by the law, I think the pope's cousin had an egg farm or something, thus eating eggs were ok), and pasta.

Lots of pasta.

Pasta with peas. Pasta with eggplant. Pasta with anything my mom found in the fridge that was still edible by Friday.

And every once in a while, we ate the peasant's dish: *Pasta c'anciovi e muddica.*

Pasta with bread crumbs and anchovy.

This delight was so good that a plenary indulgence should have been given by the pope for eating it.

Remember plenary indulgences? Are they still in existence? Pay $100, get all your sins forgiven.

Later, they were replaced by church bingo games and now finally by church raffles.

First, mom would put a little olive oil in a pan, then a few anchovies and with her fork break them up until they dissolved, which took about one minute.

Then she would place a few tablespoons of breadcrumbs in the mixture and brown the breadcrumbs.

Then she would place the mixture in a little bowl and put it on the table.

After she cooked the pasta (spaghetti), she'd put oil on the spaghetti and we would all sprinkle the bread crumbs on the spaghetti and devour it.

Mom like just a little bread crumbs. I liked a lot.

Every single time I come to Sicily, I eat this dish. Every single time.

Pasta c'anciovi e muddica.

The peasant's dish.

If the pope ever outlawed this dish, I will change religions, for sure.

My dad always told a funny joke about the outlawing of meat on Fridays.

Here is:

One day, a priest and a rabbi were riding on a plane. The priest, who was a smart-ass, said to the rabbi:

"Tell me, rabbi, in the Hebrew religion, you are not supposed to eat pork, is that correct?"

The rabbi said "Yes, that is correct. We consider the pig to be an unclean animal and we don't eat it."

The priest then said "Tell me, rabbi...between you and I...have you ever eaten pork?".

The rabbi blushed and said "Yes, once I was curious and ate a ham sandwich".

The priest smirked.

A little while later, the rabbi said to the priest:

"Tell me, father. is it true that in the Catholic religion that priest are to be celibate?"

The priest said "Yes. We give ourselves to our Lord Jesus Christ and take a vow of chastity."

The rabbi said "Tell me father...between you and I...did you ever break that vow?"

The priest blushed and said "Yes, once I took a woman."

The rabbi then said "It's a lot better than eating a ham sandwich, isn't it?"

In any case, pass the *muddica*, please.

Seven euro and twenty for a Big Mac meal at McDonald's.

That's a little over ten bucks.

For a Big Mac.

More than a whole brick oven baked pizza at a pizzeria, or a nice dish of pasta at a restaurant, or two gelatos (large), or ten espressos, or six cannoli, and a million other things.

What knucklehead would pay ten buck for a Big Mac?

Well, plenty do, as a matter of fact.

For MacDonald's and other American companies who do business in Europe, it makes plenty of sense.

They report their profits to their shareholders in dollars, so when they make a bunch of money in euro…*presto*…their profits are forty percent higher when converted to dollars…and that makes the little old lady from Iowa very happy when she gets her dividend check.

American genius.

Now, Italian kids are also getting fat too…thanks to McDonalds.

Pass those fries, please.

There are plenty of things that I often wanted to import INTO Italy that they just don't have here.

Peanut butter, for instance. Maple syrup. Decent mustard. Splenda. A better variety of cold cereals. Eggo Waffles. Potato chips (not the "Crik-Crok" brand that they sell here). Marshmallow Fluff, WD-40, decent paper towels, America coffee for the ex-pats, and a million other products that people would snap up.

How come this market isn't exploited by the Americans I often wondered?

International treaties for one…and American ignorance for the other.

Plus, Wal Mart hasn't yet polluted the continent with Chinese goods either.

In a way, custom regulations are a good way of preserving Italy's cultural identity, but I still want my peanut butter, chunky style.

A few years ago, America tried to force Italy into buying its beef made with cows that were fed genetically altered wheat. (Almost all the meat we eat in America except free range animals eat this wheat).

Italy refused…and America responded by slapping a double tariff on Italian tomato products coming into America.

Real friendly.

I think that if a clever person started an All Things American in Rome or any other big Italian city… they would clean up.

Imagine a kiosk at the Spanish steps in Rome selling American products.

Heresy, you say?

Have you seen the McDonald's there? Italy's busiest and biggest McDonald's? Yup. Right at the foot of the Spanish steps. By the way, it sells vino, too.

Big Mac with vino rosso di casa.

I'd love to see a decent Chinese restaurant here too. Not one that serves pasta instead of fried rice (as they all do). Good Chinese spare ribs… or just good ANY ribs…would do well here.

Sushi. Thai food. They would do well here too.

Better still, a doughnut shop that also sells blueberry muffins.

Or a steak house…better still, a pancake house. If IHOP is international, how come it's not in Italy?

I think an automatic car wash would clean up or an English language school actually taught by people who can speak English would do well too.

Best of all, someone who knows how to make french fries.

All Italian fries suffer a potato form of erectile dysfunction…they all droop and are soggy.

In any case, if Berlusconi or the president wish to discuss these ideas with me, I can be found at the local McDonald's holding a protest sign.

The good looking guy is me!

That Morning Java Joe (Or Java Giuseppe)

Coffee.

The elixir from God.

Is there anything better in life than that first cup of morning java?

Well, yes.

Maybe.

In America, it's the daily run to Starbuck's or Dunkin Doughnuts. Strangely, I am one of those New Englanders who drinks iced coffee twelve months a year (light, one sugar) while in America.

In Italy (especially Sicily), that is a deportable offense.

Iced coffee just hasn't cracked the culture there yet.

Even on the hottest day of the year, about the only thing that you will find is a "café freddo", which is a pre-made concoction that the barista pulls out of the refrigerator and serves it to you without ice.

Ice?

If you want ice, you specifically have to ask for it, and then you get maybe one or two cubes, if any at all.

I solved the dilemma long ago by asking for ice in a separate glass BEFORE I order the coffee or cappuccino, THEN I order the coffee.

That works.

Then, that iced cappuccino tastes the way God intended it to taste… heavenly.

By the way, the price for coffee is great too.

An espresso usually costs from sixty cents euro (about ninety cents) to seventy cents euro (about one dollar).

Governments have practically fallen when coffee prices have risen.

A cappuccino is one euro and twenty (about one dollar and fifty cents)…about 50 percent less than any American coffee chain!

Why?

Well, because coffee is part of the culture…an entrenched part of the mindset.

Teas can be found. So can de-caf coffee. But really, who drinks tea at a bar in Sicily?

Sicilians like to buy their fruits and veggies fresh every day from their local roadside stand. This farmer is selling fruit from his nearby farm.

No one, that's who.

Coffee beans come from Africa, Arabia, and South America.

The African coffee bean, with its rich dark flavor and lovingly roasted by master Sicilian companies, is flat out the best there is.

In Giarre, a quaint little town between Catania and Taormina, is located the Ionia Coffee Company, which is, in my opinion, the world's best coffee.

I have imported this brand several times and when I have none left in the warehouse, I frantically try to come up with a substitute…but they all are a distant second to this heavenly brew.

Another great coffee from Sicily is Torrisi Café which I also adore.

Generally, Italian supermarkets are well stocked with many different brands of coffee…except, of course, American coffees.

Once a week, different coffee brands are placed on sale with prices ranging from one dollar and twenty five cents to five dollars for a half pound bag.

Still, coffee in the morning is my "raison d'être" when in Sicily.

Brew yourself a cup in your espresso maker and take that precious elixir outside and sit in the sunshine and magically you will be taken to a different place.

Coffee is duty free too. It is always a good idea to buy several packages and throw them in your luggage. They travel well and will remind you when you are back in the states that you once experienced heaven.

Coffee.

That magic, romantic elixir that God sent to earthlings just to give them a glimpse of what heaven is like. Really, I believe that.

It wasn't until I was nine years old that I learned that Christmas trees were supposed to have a nice graceful crown on top.

I always thought that you were supposed to saw the top off and make it flat.

That's what my dad did each and every year.

I also thought that moms and dads were supposed to argue while putting up the tree and that you were supposed to put so much stuff on the tree that by the day before Christmas it was dead and that piles of needles were everywhere.

Ahh...the annual Christmas tree affair at the Zappalà household.

Repeated thousands of times yearly across every Italian household in America.

What memories.

Right after Thanksgiving every year, dad would lug into the house this huge frozen thing that was green.

His "friend" as he told us, saved him the "fullest" and "biggest" tree every year.

All bundled up like a green popsicle.

For three days it would sit there on our living room floor defrosting, branches popping out one by one.

The logical mind would tell you to mount the tree BEFORE it thawed out and put it on the stand, but not at my house. Here, the tree had to thaw out on the carpet, and then a struggle had to take place as you put in on the stand.

The Sicilian Way.

Of course, dad always bought a fourteen foot high tree, except that the ceiling in the house was only ten feet high.

That meant that the four foot crown on top always got sawed off, and we always had a flat-topped tree.

Mom used to go nuts.

Every year.

I always thought that you were supposed to be in awe that the tree was so "full" too, despite the fact that every year at least one side of the tree had virtually no branches.

Plus, I remember the wires protruding from the middle of the tree and nailed into two corners of the wall to "help" it stay straight.

This ritual, of just putting up the tree, was the first night's family activity.

You were supposed to tell your husband that he was crazy, according to family tradition.

Then, the tree had to "set" for a full twenty four hours so it could "breathe".

DAY TWO of the Rite of the Christmas Tree consisted of putting between twenty to thirty strings of lights on each and every branch.

From the flat-topped crown he would start, and work his way down. Branch by branch, inch by inch, with mom holding him by the waist as he leaned over while standing on the kitchen chair.

I also thought that many brown extension cords were part of the Rite too, as at least seven of them were connected to those strings of lights and then further connected to every outlet in three rooms by even more extension cords.

With the LIGHTING OF THE TREE CEREMONY, the evening's activities were concluded, leaving only two nights left for this annual sacred tradition.

DAY THREE was the ceremonial placing of the "bulbs" on the tree. Not ornaments "bulbs".

God forbid if one was broken. God forbid if mom couldn't find all the "hooks".

By the end of DAY THREE, with each branch now drooping so much that they were circular, we'd be told to go to bed as the last sacred rite, the "Placing of the Tinsel" was a sacred ADULT right.

On the morning of DAY FOUR, we'd scurry down the steps from our bedroom to see this lead-covered, silver encrusted, tinsel-tree standing there.

"Thirty boxes," dad would proudly say.

That evening, with Patti Page, Doris Day, Nat King Cole playing on the 33RPM mono-recorded "record-player" (again strictly off limits to children), the tree would be lit for the first time…resplendent in all its glory.

These two adorable tykes are me and my brother Tommy the year that cowboy and Indian outfits were a popular Christmas fad. Note the cardboard fireplace in the background. That was popular back then too!

"Honey" mom would say, "I think this is the most beautiful tree ever".

Dad would give her that knowing glance as he stooped over to water that poor thing for the fourth time that day.

In any case, by Christmas Day, pine needles littered the living room as the beautiful tree was in the last stages of its death throes.

"Next year" dad would say, "I think we will get an artificial tree. They just came out this year."

Mom would raise her eyebrows a bit and say "Anything you want, dear."

I never understood why she rolled her eyes though.

The Rite of The Christmas Tree.

Another sacred Sicilian tradition.

I have been fortunate enough to have eaten great food from all over the world.

Over the years, I spent a great deal of time traveling far and wide… from Tokyo to Amsterdam… and just about every place in between. I have eaten local cuisine in Italy, France, England, Belgium, Japan, Holland, Canada…and of course in many states in America.

Then there is Sicily.

For this love letter to *Sicilia Bedda*, I treat her as a country simply because regular "Italians" know that her cuisine surpasses anything they can offer.

I say this too after eating everywhere in Italy.

Consider the *arancini di riso*, the rice ball.

The simplest of fare. Made from the simplest of ingredients…bread-crumbs, rice, and either white (with creamy béchamel) or red (with *sugu*, peas, chicken). From Palermo to Messina you can find them at every bar. From Palermo to Messina, eating only one will placate the soul…as it has done for centuries now.

Consider the *scacciata*…the noble *scacciata*…(meat pie) filled with sausage or cheese, or vegetable…or anything else really…made by legions of Sicilian wives and mothers and perhaps is the reason Sicilian men don't leave their mom's house until they are forty.

Or perhaps a *pizza*? From Sicily? That wood-fired, brick-oven gift from heaven with a choice of over fifty different varieties on which to choose. Again the simplest of ingredients…flour, tomatoes, cheese, a little oil… merge into a unity with your spirit.

Feeling down today? Then you need a *crispeddi di ricotta* (*crispeddi* with ricotta)or maybe a *crispeddi di acciughi*…(*crispeddi* with anchovy) or just one covered in sugar or honey.

Carbohydrates for the soul.

Main dishes? *Pesce spada* (swordfish), *Agnello* (lamb), *Pesce bianco* (white fish), anchovies, sardines, lobster, prawns, *vongole* (clams), beef? Or perhaps *stucco, nero di seppia*? Or countless varieties of pasta?

Watching your calories? Then how about some fresh fruit? Oranges, lemons, apples, peaches, cherries, mulberries, apricots, *nespole, fichi d'india*, watermelon, cantaloupe, honey dew-melon? Just to cleanse the pallet.

Almost all organic too. Did you know that ninety percent of Sicily's soil would be considered organic in America?

You are a vegetarian perhaps? Welcome to *Vegetarian Heaven*. Mushrooms, broccoli, cauliflower, onions, lettuce, rabe, tomatoes (technically classified as a fruit), potatoes, asparagus, (green and white), peas, beans, legumes, radicchio, eggplant, peppers...are just a few those come to mind. Take your pick.

There are over fifty more vegetables grown from the Sicilian soil.

Ah...you want sweets. How about a *cannoli* (with boiled cream, chocolate, pistachio, or ricotta)? Maybe a *cassata siciliana* cake? *Gelati*? *Granita*?

We have it all.

Of course, in every province you travel...from Messina to Trapani... you will find hundreds of mutations of sweet things.

Sicilians have a sweet tooth.

How about an *ossa di morti* (literally: "dead man's bones") on All Souls Day? Or maybe a *minni di virgini* (literally: "breast of the virgin") on The Feast of Saint Agatha? Or perhaps a *aceddu ccu l'ovu*...those wonderful bird-shaped biscotti with a hardboiled egg built right into them for Easter?

Cheese? Hard, soft, semi-soft? We have two hundred varieties to choose from. All made the original way.

The ancient way.

Then there is the wine. And *grappa*. There are literally hundreds of varieties of both. Perhaps you desire a "sweet" wine? Have you tried the Marsala wine? And of course, afterwards there is the herb flavored aperitif *Amaro*. Almost every province has their variety. I prefer the Averna brand myself.

Renowned the world over.

The cuisine in Sicily evolved over the centuries of brutal occupation by the various conquering peoples and the Sicilians took the best each occupier had to offer and eventually adopted it as their own, even changing the basic recipes to suit their needs.

Today, chefs from all over the world regularly offer Sicilian-based cuisine in their restaurants.

As a matter of fact, one of the best "Sicilian" restaurants that I have ever eaten in was in Tokyo. That's Japan.

I remember that evening well. It was in the Rapongi section of Tokyo and I had gone there with friends. It was a refreshing change, to tell you the truth, because by that time Sushi was coming out of my ears. I desperately needed some familiar food for my souls, and I thought that Italian food, even in Japan, MIGHT have a semblance to what I wanted.

Believe me, the food was spectacular. If I closed my eyes, I would have sworn that I was in Italy.

All the chefs were Italians and most of the wait staff too. The meal (though profoundly expensive for a regular Italian restaurant) was really a five star meal. It was simply wonderful.

After finishing that meal fit for a Sicilian Prince, I asked to see the owner. A Japanese man introduced himself to me as the owner.

He told me that he had gone to Sicily many times to study the cuisine and decided to make a Sicilian restaurant in Japan.

He imported every single item…from door locks to tables from Sicily.

He brought in Sicilian tradesmen to build the ovens for pizza. He used only Sicilian chefs. He flew in tuna daily from Sicily to make his sushi (hey…we are in Japan, right?) and generally cloned a magnificent place …seven thousand miles away.

Best of all, after this spectacular meal, each customer was offered a fine Cuban cigar to go with their grappa or port wine. A Cohiba cigar… the world's finest hand-rolled cigar…with a wonderful glass of Marsala after dinner…it just doesn't get any better than that!

Scores of people have written wonderful cookbooks about Sicilian cuisine and most of them are very good.

However, I think I have the best one.

Shortly before mom died back in 2009 at age 90, she wrote down all the recipes that her mom had given her and put them into book form for all the grandchildren.

My sister Anna helped her put them together. Mom hand-wrote the recipes and their ingredients, and Anna had them reproduced and designed a wonderful little cover. That Christmas all the children and grandchildren

Tokyo has some of the world's best Sicilian restaurants…really!

received one as a Christmas present. What a wonderful gift.

Those little books were one of her last Christmas presents to us all.

In tribute to her, on Christmas Eve 2009 and also for 2010 and I imagine every year going forward, members of my family now make one of those seventeen recipes and in doing so the spirit of mom and "nana" will be with us every holiday season.

After all, that's the Sicilian way.

Food, we were taught, is not merely for eating. "Real" food, prepared by someone in the family for others in the family is a way of showing love for those members. Sitting around the dinner table and sharing that experience completes the circle.

Thus, a family meal…although it is "food" technically…is really much much more. It is an extension of love.

Mom taught us well.

Looking at my waistline though…too well!

The Peddler

Every time I go for an espresso in Viagrande, there is this old man standing in front of the café selling his wares.

Seems like I have seen this man there for years, really.

He hangs around in front of the café every day with a cart-like contraption that he built at least fifty years ago.

It is made of wood and has four wheels.

On top is a flat area that he displays his wares. It has two handles that he lifts and pushes when he is ready to go home.

He has on display and for sale every cheap item from China imaginable; pens, lighters, tiny screw drivers to fix your glasses, cheap tools, cheap plastic children's toys and the like.

Mostly junk.

Sicilian Dollar Store style junk.

Everything is on sale, however, for whatever you want to pay for it... fifty cents, seventy five cents...it doesn't matter.

I love this old man. To me, he is Sicily. He is thin and usually unshaven. His belt is far too big and a good portion of it is doubled looped through his pants. He wears a Sicilian" "coppula"...a "cappidduzzu" as my grandfather called it...on his head. A cigarette dangles from his mouth. He has an old, mountain-weathered face. He looks every bit his eighty-five years of age.

He is from the hills somewhere; probably Trecastagni, Zafferana, Sant'Alfio or any number of towns leading to Etna.

Wearing that weather-beaten cap, boots worn out decades ago, woolen trousers worn summer or winter topped with suspenders and a long sleeve cotton shirt, he is a splendid sight.

The original Old Man of the Mountain.

The Peddler.

The lines on his face tell of a once strong man; a farmer perhaps. The callus-covered hands tell of sweat and toil. This man has seen much, I think to myself.

Now, as he approaches the end of a lifetime of labor, here he is...

selling cheap Chinese imports on a wooden table in a small Sicilian town located near a volcano.

I always buy a trinket or two. Sometimes I buy many.

I never take the trinkets away with me.

Who would? That is not why I put my money down. Not for the trinkets. Rather, for the Peddler.

I engage him in conversation. He speaks the ancient Sicilian dialect, not Italian.

He speaks like my grandfather. I understand him perfectly, clearly.

He tells me of the five children all grown up and married off. All on the mainland. He has a small plot of land not far away. His wife passed on years ago. All he has left is what you see on the table.

This is the backside of Sicily. The side not shown on any itinerary.

Look closer, and there are others.

In Sicily, this is one of the results of sixty-seven governments that have risen and fallen since the end of the Second World War. The tidal wave of money that leaves Rome always arrives in Sicily as a trickle.

Abject poverty, Sicilian style.

The safety net that we have in America is not as strong in Sicily and Italy. Italy chronically is near the brink of insolvency and a result, there are many Peddlers throughout the Island.

In Acireale are the Africans from Morocco and now the Tunisians and Libyans. They line the sidewalks leading to the Duomo. Their wares are displayed on blankets that are placed on the sidewalk. Cheap sunglasses mostly. Rip-off designer bags. All for a few euro. Other sell African wooden figures or pop art from Egypt painted on papaya. Others sell Moroccan rugs.

Everything has a price.

They live in cramped apartments in Catania…often ten or twenty to a small three room flat.

Still, to them, this is heaven.

Can you imagine that?

Then there are the washers. Teams of men and teens from Morocco who occupy almost every intersection of every busy street waiting for the stop light to change to red, at which point they offer to wash your windshield for fifty cents.

They live in the shadows. The shadows of heaven.

In Taormina are the Gypsies, begging with their infant for a coin or two.

On the beaches are the Chinese offering a massage for fifteen euro… right on the spot.

The old man with the push cart, the street vendors, the window washers, the Gypsies, the Chinese…and many other people from far off and exotic lands are in Sicily for a purpose…to live.

Just live. Nothing more.

Sicilians, being who they are, understand. They too understand oppression, poverty, and those seeking to find a better life.

Only when there is a sensational act of violence…not very often…do the newspapers raise a hue and cry. Mostly though, life plods on.

Just as it has for centuries.

That peddler up in Viagrande isn't the first to hawk his wares there. He's been there for centuries, hasn't he?

And he will be there for centuries more.

That is what Sicily has always been…a refuge of sorts…for the oppressed.

Welcoming them, too.

She understands.

Forget Hertz, Avis, Budget, or Eurocar.

Forget all those national and international car rental outfits that want to rent you sleek new cars. For me, there is only one place to rent a car in Catania...Volcano Car Rental...located in a field outside of Catania close to the Sigonella Naval Base....and home to the love in my life....my "new" 1997 jet black four cylinder slightly dented Ford Fiesta...The Black Stallion.

I heard about Volcano Car Rental from a friend.

I was told that you could rent an ugly duckling beat up used car for less than half price of the national car rental outfits, so I decided to check it out.

A week before I arrived, I had Massimo track down the owner of the company, a nice guy by the name of Calogero. Massimo told me to wait on the sidewalk at a certain location at the airport when I arrived and he'd find me.

He did.

Driving a dust covered 1995 Opel Cadet, he zipped around, greeted me, and threw the luggage into his chariot. "We have to go back to the agency," he told me, "to sign the papers."

Looking at the two guys that were in the back seat, I wondered if I was going back to Volcano Car Rental or was I going to be thrown INTO a volcano. Not knowing what I was getting into, I said to myself, "why not" and jumped in.

Off we went.

The drive took about twenty minutes, and Calogero and I talked on the way to the agency. Calogero was a nice man. He told me that after he married an American woman they settled in Catania to raise their family.

He bought and sold beat up old cars. He sold them usually to American servicemen on the nearby military base.

Since the servicemen were in Sicily for only a couple years at a time, they were interested in basic transportation...something that could get them from point "A" to point "B" safely.

So, that is what he sold...beat up old jalopies that still had a little life in them....just what I needed.

"I fix them all," he said. "They all run good. They are a little banged up, but they will get you where you want to go."

Arriving near the front gate of Sigonella, located on the right hand side close to the main entrance, in a grass field enclosed by a chicken wire fence and wood gate, is the famous Volcano Car Rental.

Unlocking the gate and swinging it open, we entered.

There, in front of my eyes, was a scene so hilarious that I almost laughed out loud... his inventory of vehicles.

All six of them.

None born after 1997. All at least fourteen years old. An Opel. A Fiat Punto. Another Punto. A Nissan. Two other cars whose make was impossible to identify.

Then I saw it.

In the field to the right...just beyond that clump of weeds. The new love of my life.

The Black Stallion. My slightly used, slightly battered, slightly dented and scratched 1997 Ford Focus four cylinder, with a missing passenger mirror, no pads on the gas pedal, clutch, or break...sitting there in all its beauty.

"That one," I said.

"Start it up," I said.

Calogero was hesitant. "Can you handle such a car?" he asked. Clenching my jaw, I nodded. My sweaty palms were eager with anticipation. "Turn that motor over," I said.

Fishing around a bucket of old car keys, he found the Stallion's key.

Not waiting for him, I snatched the keys and jumped in.

Eager with anticipation and with that dry lump in my throat, I placed the key in the ignition and turned it.

VROOM...VROOM...VROOM....

It not only started up, it was purring like a...stallion.

Wiping off the accumulated dirt that has caked on the front window and pulling up a few weeds that looked like they were growing into the motor, I popped this beauty into reverse and got him going.

He shook his head and neighed. His muscles, long unused, flexed.

He was free at last to ride the wind once again. I wished I had a carrot to feed him, I thought.

The bond was instantaneous. The Black Stallion and I.

Brought together by destiny and fate.

In any event, I made a deal with Calogero. 17 euro a day. Including insurances, taxes, everything.

Plus, the 500 euro fee…I was renting the Stallion for 30 days…would all be applied to the purchase price. All I needed to do was hand the guy another 300 euro and the Stallion was mine.

For 800 euro, I had the car of my dreams. A 1997 Ford Focus with 140,000 kilometers on it. It wasn't old…it was "experienced" I thought.

On the highway, she roared to life.

Zipping down the breakdown lane at a cool 45 MPH, I passed a couple of Vespa motor scooters and a guy pushing a car.

Man, can he fly, I thought.

In any event, I am one happy camper.

I know that as time passes that we will develop a unity of spirit and that he will probably anticipate my every move, my every thought.

Back in America, I have owned sleek new Lincolns, Toyotas, and other luxury vehicles, but never ever have I been so fortunate to own such a wonderful and magnificent machine as my Black Stallion.

God, I am so lucky!

It struck me hard, fast and unexpectedly.

During a routine physical exam two weeks before I was to leave for Sicily, an abnormal EKG caused my doctor alarm.

"Alfred," she said. "I do not like what I see here. I want you to go immediately for blood work and a stress test. I think you may have suffered some sort of cardiac event, and it needs to be immediately addressed."

Me?

Hercules?

Something wrong with my heart? Impossible!

A stress test and blood work, followed by a few other tests confirmed the worst…I had in fact suffered a "cardiac event"…a silent one…and I had two blocked arteries to boot!

Before my mind and emotions could get wrapped around what I was being told…after all, I was feeling great…I was placed in an ambulance and whisked to Boston where I had two stents placed in my heart to clear the blockages.

Overnight, my life had been turned upside down. My kids were beside themselves with fear. Their rock of life suddenly cracked.

Processing my life as I lay in the hospital bed, I should have seen something coming…especially at my age.

When I was a young man I was an athlete. I played all sorts of sports. As the years passed, I gained weight. I picked up the smoking habit. I entered a high stress profession…the legal profession…and I didn't watch what I ate.

Basically, I lived a rat-pack type of fast life…and now the chickens had come home to roost.

The perfect storm for a cardiac event.

Thankfully, my doctors told me that the blockages were clear…but that I needed to watch my diet, exercise, stop smoking (I had in fact stopped smoking three weeks before all the commotion thank God), stay on the medication that they gave me, and most importantly, change my lifestyle and eliminate the unnecessary stress in my life.

Me. The Warrior. The Alpha Male.

Change or die, I was told.

Benched by the Great Coach in the Sky.

After discharge from the hospital I decided to follow his instructions to the letter. I had my grandkids to consider…I want them to have a grandfather…not to mention my kids who still needed guidance.

Plus, I had a lot more to do before packing it in, so I decided that all this trauma was a solid wake up call for me…not the end of the world.

In any event, a follow up exam a few days later cleared me to go to Sicily, and off I went.

Fortunately, I have a good network of friends in Sicily, with Massimo being at the top of the list. I knew that if anything were ever to happen, I was in friendly territory with trusted friends who would look after me.

I landed in Sicily wiser and on the path to a (hopefully) longer and healthier life.

The morning after I arrived, I headed to Aci Castello with my walking shoes on, my IPOD, my cap, and my work out clothes.

I walked the coast for forty five minutes. My exercise regimen began anew…in Sicily.

I followed the sea. I breathed the sea air. I closed my eyes when I walked and inhaled the fragrance scent of the budding Sicilian flowers that were exploding everywhere.

Funny, smoking kills the sense of smell, doesn't it?

Now, I can breathe. Now I can smell scents that I haven't smelled in decades. I smell red, pink, and yellow, purple. I smell orange, lemon, and lilac. I smell green.

I walked. I walked more. Life returned to my being. My soul began to re-generate… I moved…I moved some more. Life began to return with every step.

For the next five week, I re-created myself. Every morning I got up early, put on my sneakers and walked the Sicilian coast. I meditated. I cleansed my body of a lot of toxins that it contained…both physical toxins and emotional toxins…that accumulated as the years passed.

I watched my diet. I stopped and smelled the roses, as they say.

Everyday, I felt better and better. The weight began to drop. The blood pressure was normal. I was feeling like a teenager again.

Sicily is a wonderful place to recuperate from a "cardiac event" as they say.

The climate, the cuisine, and the people were my doctors and nurses. I did watch what I eat: fish, fruit and vegetables would be my staples in life going forward, and what better place to find these things?

It looks like someone (I know who…believe me), gave me a second chance here.

I do not know how many quality years I can squeak out of this body of mine. However, I promise myself that I will give it my best shot, and that Sicily is the place for it.

Life is short I am told. I heard that expression but never stopped to contemplate its meaning.

Now, I understand. Tomorrow, and every day after, I will walk by the sea again. I cannot imagine life without Sicily. It made me a re-born man when I first discovered her joys. Now, years later she nourishes me; heals me.

Bedda Sicilia.

Grazie a Dio.

A. Prelude

I am waiting for the police to come and visit me.

I have been waiting for four days actually. Will they ever come?

No, I am not a criminal; I am not wanted by them. When will they be here, I wonder?

No, there is no emergency, nothing is wrong.

Well, why am I waiting for the cops to visit me in my home…in Sicily?

It's just that this morning I officially registered my residence in Sicily, and part of the process is that the police have to come and check out my place…just to make sure that I live here and am not a fiction.

Massimo, as usual, helped me with the initial phase with the process, which required going to the Municipal Offices and filling out basic paperwork.

I conned him yet again into wasting a morning of his life to assist me in registering Sicily as my official residence with Sicilian authorities.

However, I think that today he was very happy to assist me on this project as he knew how much it meant to me.

Today, I "officially" registered with the Commune of Aci Catena and declared Aci Catena as my residence.

The first thing I had to do was have all my documents in order… which I did. Birth certificate, Italian passport, everything was in order.

Off we went to Aci Catena to find the municipal offices.

The town clerk's office was our first step in the process, when Massimo told the clerk that I wanted to register Aci Catena officially as my residence in Sicily, the clerk asked incredulously "why?"

As in…why would someone from America want to move to Sicily… shouldn't it be the other way around?

Well, no.

I want to reverse immigrate. I want to come home in the purest sense.

Which is what we told her. She smiled and actually began to flirt with me.

Geez.

In any event, she was very helpful. She helped fill out a bunch of papers. Just one more bunch to go she said.

Step one, complete. I was handed a paper and told to go to the tax office.

There I had to register for taxes (gulp). Included in this department was the annual charge for garbage pickup of two hundred ten euro which everyone pays.

Of course I want to pay for garbage pickup I thought. I just wish they would actually pick it up once in a while.

After completing the form and handing it to the clerk, he asked me "Why would you move here? You live in America." Again I told the story.

Again the incredulous look.

Well, the next step in the process is an official visit from the police. They must come to make sure that I am real.

"When will they come?" I ask. "When they want to," I am told.

"Am I supposed to just stay home and wait for them?" I ask.

"If you want to complete the residency requirement" I am told.

Hmm.

"Usually, they visit in the mornings," I am told.

"OK, I guess I have no choice then," I say.

"Correct. Here…give them this paper to sign. When they sign it, bring it back to us along with three passport photos of yourself and we'll give you your identity card."

So, here I sit waiting for the cops to come.

Why am I doing this again?

Oh yeah…so I can live here.

Guess I'll have to wait, then.

In the meantime, I need to study for my driver's exam…in Italian… so I can get a license.

Now that should be a barrel laughs, for sure!

Geez.

B. The Visit By The Police

I waited for four days for the police to come. I was told that they do these visits in the mornings, so I really didn't kill four whole days waiting for the policeman... Just four half days.

When he arrived, he was a very nice man. I had my next door neighbor come over to translate for me just in case I didn't understand something.

However, he was nice.

He stuck his head into a few rooms and commented what a nice place it had.

He sat down at the kitchen table and completed a form and had me sign it.

He kept the original and gave me a copy. He told me that now all I had to do was return the form to the municipal offices and I would be able to get my identity card.

After he left, I looked at that form.

Everything had gone so smoothly, I thought. I am one step away from really accomplishing my goal.

By tomorrow I will officially be a citizen of a Sicilian town.

Honestly…joy overcame me.

I guess I became a little emotional.

Re-discovering my cultural identity has been a long process, and it seemed like the process of self identity was almost complete.

C. The Home Stretch: Getting My Identity Card.

The next morning I got up bright and early and headed to La Zagara, the nearby shopping center in Valverde. La Zagara had one of those photo machines that for three euro you sit behind a curtain and have a passport picture taken.

I figured out how to have the photos taken and I headed to the Municipal offices along with the form that was given to me by the policeman.

On the way over, I stopped by the local pastry shop and picked up some cookies. I figured that since everyone was so nice to me helping me fill out all the forms, that today I would treat the whole clerk's office to some nice pastry.

When I arrived, the same clerk greeted me and she was astounded that I would bring cookies for her and the whole office.

I guess no one does that. However, I felt it was the least I could do.

I gave her the signed form receipt, the passport photos and in half an hour she called my name and gave my Italian identity card.

When I looked at it, I really couldn't believe what I was seeing.

Against all odds, I had done everything necessary that there was to do and had obtained my card.

By Italian law, I now had to carry this with me at all times. This document is the controlling document within Italy for all her citizens, and now I was officially counted as one of her own.

One thing I have to do now is buy a bigger wallet. It is slighter bigger that a credit card in size and I don't want to bend it or get it dirty.

Well, I did it. I am official.

Good job, Alfred!

This was something I simply had to do.

One week ago, I was a patient at Saint Elizabeth's Hospital in Boston getting ready to be discharged after having two arteries in my heart unblocked with stents...and now I find myself today on a side street in Trecastagni, parking my 1997 eight foot long Ford Fiesta in a space eight foot and three inches long.

The reason: today was the annual feast day of my patron saint...Saint Alfio....and I had made the trek up here to thank him and his brothers for interceding on my behalf over my recent health issue.

Saint Alfio and his two brothers Filadelfo and Cirino had been martyred by the Romans back in the third century AD, and this town never forgot. For fifteen years now I have made this pilgrimage and nothing was going to stand in the way.

I was feeling better and better with each passing day leading up to the festival, and despite the very windy weather and rain the night before, I decided to take a chance and make the drive up the mountain.

Zipping up the mountain a million times these last fifteen years, I now know every nook and cranny of her ways including how to zigzag around traffic and find a parking space when none exists. However, remembering that last New Year's Eve that I nearly drove off the mountain road due to the thick fog, I learned the hard way to never take Etna's roads for granted.

Today wasn't going to be a long visit: I wanted to see the Three Saints come out of the church (where thousands of people were patiently waiting to see them) and then go into the church and say a quick silent prayer.

I usually like to be alone on this day, as this is the day that I remember all my ancestors and their sacrifices.

After parking the car, I picked my way through the crowd and headed for the church.

I passed stall after stall selling everything imaginable: nuts, food, knick-nacks, CDs, religious things, household things, shoes, furniture, bunches of fresh garlic, crispelle, barbecued horse-meat sandwiches, *sasizza* (sausage) sandwiches, votive candles, coconuts, balloons, toys, hats, dishes and kitchen gadgets. These are but a few of the wares that were for sale today in stands lining both sides of the streets for nearly a half mile as I slowly picked my way through the crowd.

Learning the lessons of the past, when I come to these tightly-packed events I travel light, meaning that I leave the wallet at home and have twenty euro hidden somewhere…usually in my shoe.

I know many a friend who had his pocket picked during this walk to the church, and I wasn't going to join that group.

I made the walk and found a place to observe the upcoming festivities. At any moment, the statues of the three saints, mounted on the "vara" which would be pulled through the streets by the faithful, would appear to the roar of the crowd.

The anticipation was building.

I had witnessed this exact moment many times and as I waited for them to appear, I looked up at the sky…which was now clear and sunny… and said thanks to God for allowing me to be here.

Within seconds the *vara* appeared to the roar and delight of the crowd.

Seated atop the *vara*, in majestic splendor, were the three ancient statues of the slain brothers.

Scores of people then began handing infants to the priests who were on top of the *vara*.

The infants were wearing a red garment and the priest took this garment as an offering.

Others gave money. Others prayed. Still others just milled around enjoying the spectacle.

Then, the fireworks started.

Day time fireworks. Beautiful burst of colored fireworks…visible even in the sunlight…started and continued for fifteen minutes.

From the church steeple, confetti and paper streamers were released, and a helicopter circled overhead dropping rose pedals on the crowd.

A huge banner affixed with the images of the three saints and attached to enormous balloons was released into the sky toward heaven.

Really, it was a wonderful sight full of religious fervor and symbolism and I was so happy to be able to witness it.

After twenty minutes, the boys pulling the *vara,* which was attached to long ropes began their task, and the vara slowly began to move away

My patron saints…Alfio, Cirino and Filadelfo at the Church of Sant Alfio in Trecastagni.

from the church toward one of the throng-filled streets.

Once the crowd began to thin in front of the church, I made my move.

Entering the church, I found a spot in a pew.

I thanked Saint Alfio and his brothers for interceding for me hundreds of times in the past year. I lit candles for my parents, grandparents, and loved ones.

Mostly though, I contemplated my life.

I know I ducked a bullet this year. Only a chance comment with my doctor as I was leaving her office had compelled me to take that EKG in the first place.

Had I not taken that EKG, the two sticks of dynamite in my heart could have blown at any second.

Saint Alfio was looking out for me that day.

I know it.

He interceded with God on my behalf and saved my hide.

I needed to thank him and the boys.

Yesterday, I did.

I haven't a clue how health care is supposed to be paid for in America.

The only thing that I know for certain is that if someone is sick and needs medical attention, then they should be treated.

That's the Christian thing to do.

The issue in the states is a political football, kicked around endlessly by every talking head on the television.

I have had experiences with hospitals in America, Holland, and Sicily...and Sicily ranks far behind in my view.

While I am sure that there are excellent doctors in Sicily, in the final analysis if something catastrophic were to happen to me while I am here, I would try to get either to Milan (where there are some of Europe's best hospitals) or back to the states.

I don't think I would let a Sicilian doctor treat me for a major condition.

The first hurdle is the language barrier.

In America, I have a hard enough time trying to follow a doctor's advice in English, forget Italian.

If I have to be treated by an Italian (Sicilian) doctor, then a translator would be necessary...one who knows exactly what the doctor is saying, and explains it to me in a way that I can understand it.

That last thing I would want is an important issue getting lost in translation.

The next hurdle is the hospitals in Sicily themselves.

Corruption (translate: Mafia involvement) is rife in urban centers, and that includes hospitals. Recently, a sleek new hospital in Catania opened. It took many years to build and was grossly over budget. It was also discovered that if an earthquake were to occur, it would probably collapse.

The reason? The firm supplying the concrete to the hospital used far too much sand in the mixture of sand to concrete to build the thing, and now it has been declared unsafe. (By the way, this same firm also built many overpasses on the *autostrada*).

Thus, shoddy construction of the physical facilities is a major concern to me.

How about the care at a public hospital in Sicily? Would you believe me if I told you that if a patient wanted a glass of water...he better well have brought a bottle himself as water is not provided to patients? How's that?

Usually, the families of the patients must provide necessities...water... food...johnnies. slippers...unlike the American hospitals.

In Sicily, there is essentially two types of care given: those at public clinics and hospitals...where the care is shoddy, incomplete and of the hold your breath variety, and then at private clinics and private hospitals...generally far better in facilities and general overall quality, including professional staff. However, private clinics are not covered by nationalized health programs.

For these private clinics and hospitals, a patient either purchases private insurance or pays cash on the barrel.

Thus, for three reasons...language, facilities, and general quality of care, in a dire emergency I would think seriously about Milan or Rome for my needs...or head back to America.

At the top of this piece I mentioned Holland.

Holland is cutting edge, and many lessons in America could be learned if the Dutch methods were studied by the Americans.

In a previous life, a decade and a half ago, I had the good fortune to meet a wonderful Dutch woman and marry her.

Unfortunately, she suffered three devastating brain aneurysms while visiting her parents in Amsterdam, and I was forced to negotiate the Dutch health care system while my wife lay in a coma near death.

While I won't go into the specific details of the trauma she suffered and the resulting demise of our marriage a few years later, what I do remember is how the Dutch cared for her...and for me.

I doubt that in America I could have received such treatment.

Their hospitals were clean, state of the art, cutting edge. Their doctors bi-lingual and confident. They knew what the problems were and the probable outcome.

Juxtaposing the three health care systems against one another, I think the Dutch system (nationalized by the way) is superior to the other two.

Recently I had a heart issue that surfaced during a routine exam that resulted in me having two stents placed in my heart at Saint Elizabeth's

Hospital in Boston. The treatment was beyond first rate. Unbelievable, actually.

In one day I was up and about.

Five days later, I was in Sicily.

Telling this story to Massimo, he told me a story about his late father in law. When his father in law was ill with a heart problem, he was brought to a clinic in Sicily and had a couple of stents placed in his heart. He ended up a month later going to Milan and having them replaced by doctors there who were not impressed by the work they saw.

Thus, I have a choice to make, and I now know what direction I am headed.

First of all, I will try to eat better, eliminate the bad stuff, exercise, eliminate stress and fill my head with positive thoughts.

Then, I will interview a few doctors here in Sicily, and hopefully find one or two that I have confidence in.

However, that doctor will be in communication with my US doctors, and between them, maybe I can come up with a plan.

Here's the point: an ounce of prevention is worth a pound of cure, and I will be prepared.

No doubt.

Keeping It Simple
and on the Table

The news was harsh but I must heed the message.

Years of hard living had finally caught up with me and my doctor told me in no uncertain terms that I had to steer another course immediately...or else.

"Alfred, you dodged a bullet. I was able to open up the two blocked arteries in your heart, but you have to make some fundamental changes in your life concerning diet, exercise, stress management, taking your meds and generally chill out. The decision is yours: follow my advice and you can live another twenty five years. Ignore my advice and all bets are off."

At age sixty, finally, someone got my attention.

It's not that I have a fear of dying. Lord knows that He has blessed me with more than I am entitled to, and I have really lived a full and rewarding life. However, there are a few things that I want to do yet, including watching my grandchildren grow up a bit, continue to offer guidance to my children, teach my beloved law students a bit more, and retire for a few years in Sicily so I can write and experience the beauty of the land.

The biggest hurdle I had overcome: I had quit smoking.

I did this after a chance visit to my doctor's office for a routine physical exam.

"Alfred," she said, "You just turned sixty, are overweight, smoke, have a stressful job and even though nothing hurts you, you are a heart attack waiting to happen."

She convinced me to take an EKG and a stress test, and before I knew it, I was in the hospital having two stents placed in my heart.

In any event, I made it through the procedure and while I was shaken to the core, I realized that the Lord had given me another chance.

I was taught long ago that I should worry about only those things I can control. In this case, I could control getting rid of the cigarettes, which I did instantaneously. Honestly, if I did go through nicotine withdrawal, I didn't notice it.

All the reading that I did about heart disease afterwards told me that fifty percent of the reason why heart disease happens is unknown, but of the remaining fifty percent, smoking is THE major culprit. Thus, simply by quitting, I was helping to improve the quality (and length) of my life.

The next step was easy too. Take your medication.

The doctors at the hospital told me that I had to take an aspirin a day for the rest of my life. Guess what? Years ago, my mom told me the same thing. When I told the doctors that I had in fact been taking an aspirin for years, they told me that since aspirin thins the blood, I probably avoided having even a more serious "cardiac event".

Thus, mom saved me once again!

In addition to the aspirin I was to take, I was told to take something for borderline high blood pressure, borderline high cholesterol, and finally a pill to get the blood flowing through the newly installed stent.

Easy I thought. Stop smoking…check. Take meds every day…check. What else?

Exercise I was told.

That's easy. I played sports in high school and college. I had been a member of a health club for years. While I had been a little neglectful with respect to working out prior to this whole mess, within a week after the procedure, I was walking first thirty minutes and then sixty minutes a day.

Snapping on the IPOD and sneakers, I re-started my morning walks.

Stop smoking. Check. Take meds. Check. Begin an exercise routine. Check.

What else?

Chill out. Work on reducing stress. Stop being a control freak. Stop being the Alpha Wolf. Take a step back. Don't sweat the small stuff. Smell the roses.

Huh?

This one was going to be a challenge.

I had sixty years of learned behavior to unlearn.

While I have many things in my life that offer me great enjoyment… writing…listening to music…reading…talking to friends and family… teaching and helping people…I was basically one big ball of nerves.

Thankfully, years ago I learned how to use breathing as a relaxation technique. I not only have to do my relaxation techinques more regularly, but I must increase the time commitment to thirty minutes a day. I must relax more.

Stress. The silent killer. I will address this one consciously and with dedication, day by day. I can do this.

I will pray and contemplate more too. I brought to Sicily with me my Sunday Missal that was given to me many years ago for my confirmation.

I love this book. I truly love this book. For years it has been on my nightstand in America and I love browsing through it.

From reading parts of the Mass in Latin (gosh, do I love Latin), to reading the Prayer of Saint Ambrose at night, to just holding the book next to my heart...it gives me strength, and calms my spirit.

Stress? Yes, I will address it.

What else?

Diet. Food. Weight.

Yikes.

However, the more I thought about it, the more I realized that being in Sicily was the perfect place to be!

Most of the stuff that I had been told to eliminate from my diet I had done long ago.

However, sometimes I slipped…and in America it is very easy to slip.

For example: Salt is now my enemy. I need to reduce salt intake to maybe 1300 mg a day.

That means getting rid of the salt shaker from the table. That means substituting herbs and spices …something that I am free to use…for salt. Thankfully, I found Mrs. Dash here…a salt substitute that people seem to like. I like it too.

In Sicily, salted snacks like chips and nuts aren't as prevalent...while they are available, it isn't central to the social diet as in the states.

Stuff that needs to be eliminated by me are creamy Caesar dressings, cheeses, cold meats, fried foods, cakes, ice cream, meats, breads and limiting my intake of olive oil.

I always thought that olive oil was a health thing to use, and it is… provided it is done in moderation.

For example: I never "measured" how much olive oil I used. Now I do. I limit myself to three tablespoons of olive oil a day.

In America, I was a "dipper"…that is, I always dipped bread in my oil that I had added salt, pepper and hot pepper…a dipping blend.

That needs to stop.

Olive oil is an oil, and all oils are fats. Not cholesterol…as cholesterol comes primarily from animal fat…but fat nonetheless.

Thus, I need to be careful in Sicily.

Fortunately, I can eat all the delicious vegetables I want.

I grill them and the variety is endless. Same with the fruit. Honestly, both vegetables and fruits taste far better here than in America.

As for bread: I need to watch myself. All the panifici make whole wheat bread (called "pane integrale") and if this bread were in America it would be a best seller. Whole wheat bread here in Sicily tastes much better than ANY bread in America.

As for pasta…I can eat it three times a week so long as I weigh it (100 grams a serving) and again use my head. Simply by tossing in fresh veggies or fresh tomatoes with garlic and herbs, I am a happy camper.

Pizza? Here the pizza in no way resembles the pizza in America. Here the pie is no more than nine inches in diameter for a small pizza. This translates into four decent size pieces. Two slices are plenty…especially since I load them up with grilled veggies…and I eliminate almost all the cheese completely. I also opt for fresh tomato as opposed to a pizza sauce and drizzle on a tiny bit of olive oil. Believe me, the pizza is something to look forward to!

Chicken and fish…no more than a couple times a week. Portion controlled too. No skin on the chicken either, and both get a generous supply of lemon juice along with herbs.

For salads, Olive oil, balsamic and a squeeze of lemon juice is wonderful…and I eat one salad a day as a meal in and of itself.

Have I given up stuff?

Sure.

French fries. Fried stuff generally. Sausage. Crispelle. Red meats. Cold cuts. Heavy deserts.

However, an occasional *granita* and *brioche* is allowed.

Most importantly, the temptations of Chinese food, McDonald's, doughnuts, Japanese food loaded with salt, or a million other convenience

The breakfast of champions: A coffee/almond granita, a brioche, and an espresso! Nothing better.

type things found in any grocery store in America…while available here… just isn't as prevalent and visible.

I think that by eating healthier I am giving myself an opportunity to re-learn proper nutritional things, which is better in Sicily than anywhere else.

So I tell myself, anyway!

Being in Sicily…away from the temptation of a franchise store on every street corner…is much better for me and my family too.

It may just give me a chance to accomplish my objectives.

Maybe.

People

1. *Marcella*

I have never met Marcella face to face. I have observed her from afar, but have never had the pleasure of meeting her.

Neither have I met her precocious little daughter Jannah.

As a matter of fact, if my universe of friends were compared to her universe of friends, I bet that of the thousands of people that know her, and of the thousands of people that know me, there is not a single one that know the both of us.

Two strangers from different locales in America (I am from the Boston area and Marcella is from the New York area), two strangers a generation apart (I am old and she is young and vibrant), and to make matters even more obtuse…we have never spoken a word to each other.

Yet, she inspires me almost every day.

For many months now, we have developed a friendship on the social network site Facebook. The singular strand in common between us is that we both have Sicilian blood coursing through our veins and somehow, we ended up an "friends" on Facebook.

Just like the other 1700 friends that I have there, and just like the other 2200 friends that she has too.

A single thread in common. Our heritage.

Or so I thought.

As is the case with Facebook, her daily posts began to cross my computer screen with a constant reference to Jannah… her daughter's name… which in Arabic means Heaven.

Curious as to who this Jannah was, I began looking forward to Marcella's daily status as it is called and hoped to learn more. I found out that Jannah had been born prematurely nearly five years ago, weighing only one pound and eight ounces.

What's more, the prospects of her survival then were slim according to the doctors as the infant had severe bleeding on the brain.

Marcella named her Jannah so she could, at least for a little while, have a piece of heaven here on earth. She has what is known as hydrophelus (fluid on the brain) child and had a shunt implanted in her brain to control the bleeding.

These last five years, she has had five different brain surgeries and the threat of the next hospital visit is not far off.

Marcella's spirit, however, is what struck me.

She has simply devoted her life to this child.

I noticed in her daily posts many things; she is witty, she is very intelligent, she is tremendously insightful and wise beyond her years. She speaks her mind on many subjects and let the chips fall where they may. I noticed that she is principled, hard working, disciplined, and sharp as a tack. I really grew to like Marcella a lot.

Mostly though, I learned what a wonderful mom she was.

She works in a pizzeria and tends bar at night to make ends meet. It looked like she works with her dad at the pizzeria and it quickly became apparent that the center of this woman's existence was this child Jannah.

Every fiber of Marcella's existence was devoted to this child.

From her daily posts, I learned that Jannah needed frequent hospitalization. It soon became apparent that some sort of seizure disorder also affected Jannah as a result of her brain issues and the doctors seemed to be having a hard time getting their arms around the problem.

It seemed that Jannah was always hospitalized and Marcella was always there at her side.

I don't think the phrase "at her side" gives Marcella sufficient justice.

It was more like "experiencing exactly what Jannah was experiencing second by second" to be honest.

For you see, I learned that the two were connected. A connection that I had never seen before. Something profoundly rare, unusual. Love at its purest. Love exactly the way the Good Lord intended it to be.

Right here on Facebook.

It became apparent to me very quickly that Marcella's center of existence…her "raison d'être" so to speak, was protecting her child and medicating her daughter with the purest form of love that I have ever witnessed. The doctors did what they had to do…but so did Marcella.

For months, I watched from afar and admired her tenacity…her "never say never" attitude.

For months I watched the ebb and flow of Jannah: some weeks she's be fine and Marcella would celebrate their daily love affair, and some weeks Jannah would return to the hospital for this test or that, and I would feel the anxiety, the hurt, the devastation, the worry between the lines in Marcella's daily posts.

Fortunately, Jannah seems to be doing terrific right now. I am convinced that the primary reason is not the doctor's care. Rather it is the mother's care and love given so unselfishly to her. Someday I hope to meet these two. The mother and the daughter.

I will tell Marcella how proud I am to know her and be of the same cultural heritage as her. I will tell her that she inspired me to combat my own illnesses. I will tell her that no matter what happens in life, she is already successful and that the Good Lord already has a place for her. I will look at Jannah too.

As I look at Jannah, I will wonder if she realizes how lucky she is. If she learns even twenty five percent of the lessons her mom taught her, she too will be successful in life.

Her mom has already taught her life's greatest lesson: the lesson of absolute love in its purest form.

I have never met Marcella or Jannah.

I hope that someday I have the good fortune to meet both of them. I would like to stare into their eyes…eyes are the gateway to the soul, you know…and I know I will see a purity of spirit with both most importantly I will get a glimpse of what Heaven is all about.

They have taught me much, and I thank them.

2. *Monsignor John Patrick Carroll-Abbing*

I remember as a young man watching Spencer Tracy and Mickey Rooney star in a terrific movie called "Boy's Town," a movie about an orphanage that the priest-character portrayed by Tracy started.

I remember the line that the priest uttered to Mickey Rooney, a homeless tough street youth who had been sent to Boy's Town but resisted getting involved in the community: "There's no such thing as a bad boy" said the priest.

Let me introduce you to a man who took the idea of this movie to a level many times higher.

Monsignor John Patrick Carroll-Abbing, the founder of Boys' Towns of Italy, Inc. way back in 1945 after the end of the World War II, and at the time an Irish priest in the Vatican Diplomatic Services, was asked by Pope Pius XII to begin a mission to help homeless and hungry children of the war develop into responsible and productive citizens.

As the Monsignor would later comment "As I put my hand on the door knob ready to leave, I suddenly realized that the Holy Father's blessing was all I had, There was no organization, no funds, no buildings, no co-workers-just a blessing."

By war's end, the American government had placed the Monsignor in charge of supervising the distribution of war relief donations from the Jewish, Protestant, and Catholic charities of the United States.

During his frequent trips to America, he began speaking ...and raising funds...for what to be his life's work...the founding and incorporation in 1951 of Boys' Town of Italy, Inc. ...and the opening of its facility for boys in the outskirts of Rome.

By 1955, Girls' Town of Rome was founded thanks to the efforts of screen star Linda Darnell and Mother Dominic Ramaccotti, a religious sister and successful university administrator from Maryland.

Thus, two entities founded Boys' Town of Rome and Girls' Town of Rome, but united under the title of Boys' Town Of Italy, Inc.

Today, these organizations offer homeless children a chance at life.

Many children are survivors of abandonment, family dysfunction, domestic violence, wars, and oppressive poverty. Today, they are prepared for life through education, career preparation, and self government.

That is the difference: Boys' Town of Italy has earned an international reputation...and is studied by many...in the manner of giving the children the opportunity to assume responsibility by becoming "citizens" of each community albeit as a storekeeper, banker, commissioner, judge or mayor... and elected by their peers!

Thousands have passed through the doors of these institutions over the years....and youngsters from Italy, Albania, Kosovo, the former Russian Republics, Ethiopia, Somalia...eighteen countries in all...have found their way to this new chance of life.

The American community has been the primary source of support funds for this organization…which has provided support for over 16,000 youngsters since its founding. There are fundraising groups throughout America working tirelessly to help.

Today, all donations are fully tax deductable and is the primary method of survival, and I think maybe you should consider supporting this organization founded by a special priest with a special vision.

Boys' Town of Italy, Inc. has offices in New York at 250 East 63rd Street, Suite 204. Tel: 212-980-8770.

Their web site is www.boystownofitaly.org

Tell them that Alfred sent you!

3. *Modern American Hero: Vincent Inserra*

Since my book *The Reverse Immigrant* was released at the end of 2010, I have been speaking to many groups about Sicily, its history, its culture, and her people.

It's what I do and it's what I enjoy. That what life is all about, right? Do what you want to do and enjoy it.

Thus, when I received an email one day from a man named Vincent Inserra from Chicago telling me how much he enjoyed reading my book and telling me that it brought back fond memories for him when he was a youngster growing up, I was happy that someone related to my writing and from that initial contact, we started an informal email relationship. Two family men that shared a mutual love: Sicily.

Corresponding by email can be somewhat difficult. After all, it is not like you are talking to a person face to face or even on the telephone. Email is black and white, sentence by sentence, thought by thought. With an email, there is no demeanor to observe, no emotion to see.

Still, we formed a friendship. Still we connected. This man had warmth and something special about him that I admired. He is a member of America's Greatest Generation I quickly learned, and was a spry octogenarian.

Thus, I was delighted to learn in one of his emails that he was the co-founder and first president of the Sicilian-American Cultural Association (SACA) of Illinois, a group which he and several others founded eighteen years ago in order to promote the good things about Sicily, and currently

Vincent Inserra and his bride of fifty-eight years, Marilyn.

serves as its Chairman of the Board.

Over the years, the members of SACA have gathered over dinner on a monthly basis and have had many presentations by people on the arts, Sicily's history, its traditions, its culture, and its image. SACA, you see, is an organization devoted to Sicily.

Every month, this dedicated group of people of Sicilian ancestry would gather at Monastero's Ristorante in Chicago, enjoy a delicious dinner prepared by the owner Joseph Monastero, and have a presentation after dinner on a special Sicilian topic.

As the years passed, the group grew, and for many members of SACA, the monthly dinner and cultural presentation was something to look forward to…a vehicle to maintain their connection to their ancestral homeland.

Chicago, as I later learned, was one of the arriving "hubs" for Sicilians back in the early twentieth century along with New York, Boston and Philadelphia.

Many of those first immigrants settled there.

Thus, I was very happy when there arrived in my inbox an invitation from Vincent to fly to Chicago and address his group.

Since I had been to Chicago many times and always enjoyed the friendly hospitality of Chicagoans, I quickly accepted. This would be a fun trip I thought to myself.

As I prepared for my departure for Chicago and as I prepared my presentation, I wondered: Who is Vincent Inserra? Why has he devoted eighteen years of his life to the promotion of Sicilian culture? What is his story? What kind of a man is he?

The results of my research were astounding.

Inadvertently, as it turns out, I had found a modern day, authentic, Sicilian-American hero who was to be admired and respected for his lifetime of accomplishment.

I felt very fortunate that Vincent has stumbled into my life. I am inspired by him and proud that he is of my blood. I am sure that as you continue reading, you will feel the same way too.

Here is what I discovered:

Vincent is a first generation Italian who was born and raised in Boston. He actually grew up in the Roxbury section of Boston, a rough and tumble section inhabited back then by arriving immigrants from everywhere.

Later in life, he settled in Chicago.

During the Second World War, he served in the Pacific Theatre as a Navy pilot, achieving the rank of lieutenant. After the war, he attended college and graduated from Boston College.

If his accomplishments in life had stopped there, in and of itself, his life was successful. A mere handful of first generation Depression era kids ever made it through high school, let alone college, and to be a Navy fighter pilot to boot...just amazing.

He was already in the top echelon of Italian-Americans of his era at this stage, but really he was just getting started.

In 1951, after graduation from Boston College, he joined the FBI as a Special Agent. He found his way to the Chicago Division of the FBI and one Sunday while in church a pretty young woman caught his eye.

Getting the courage to talk to her the following Sunday after church, he asked her name and a courtship followed, and marriage soon after.

For fifty-eight years, he has been happily married to the same wonderful and lovely woman: Marilyn.

Thus, I learned that Vincent was a Navy fighter pilot hero, a Boston College graduate, was in the FBI, and had a rock solid marriage of fifty-eight years...and counting.

But he wasn't done yet.

For twenty-five years, he rose in the ranks of the FBI. He was placed in charged of the Organized Crime and Official Corruption Squad in Chicago where he compiled an impressive record of convictions against the Chicago mob bosses and their underlings. By the time he retired from his twenty five year FBI career, Vincent's reputation as a crime-fighter was beyond reproach.

However, he wasn't done yet.

He started a second career, using his skills learned as a fraud investigator, and worked for one of the nation's largest insurance companies, a multi-billion dollar organization, as Director of Corporate Security.

For twenty-seven years, he led that organization!

Thus, this man, and considering his life's accomplishments...two profoundly successful careers...each spanning over twenty five years...would be at the top of the heap by now:

The more I learned about this hero, the more I admired.

As for civic involvement, I could write another chapter on Vincent strictly on these accomplishments. Beside SACA, he is a fourth degree member of the Knight's of Columbus, and has promoted the arts and many other civic causes.

As a family man, he has three children, three grandchildren, and three great grandchildren. The list goes on.

In other words, I had the good fortune to befriend perhaps one of the most remarkable people that I had ever met in my life, and HE asked ME to speak to his group. I was honored and humbled, to be honest with you.

In any event, I flew to Chicago eager to meet this spry and feisty gentleman and his lovely wife, and I wasn't disappointed. What friendly and remarkable people they were, and we bonded within seconds. It was if I had met old friends again.

Vincent and Marilyn picked me up at my hotel and took me to the restaurant for dinner and my presentation. On the ride over to the restaurant, meeting face to face for the first time, it was really something. I felt that I was in the presence of TWO very special and blessed people. I silently thanked the Lord for giving me this opportunity to meet such wonderful people.

At dinner, we sat together and chatted about life, about our families, about our heritage, and about things that two men who respect each other talk about. When I later gave my presentation, which I later found out went over very well, I was motivated in part because who I was talking about were people exactly like Vincent.

I was talking that evening about Sicilians who overcame insurmountable odds. I was talking that night about modern day heroes who worked tirelessly for their family and country and who were of the same cultural blood as me. In retrospect, I was talking about Vincent Inserra, someone I now aspire to emulate. An unsung hero from a generation of unsung heroes.

I am so very happy that Vincent sent me that email and invited me to Chicago after reading my book. Really, I think I would have written that book just to meet him.

I hope he invites me there to talk about the book you are reading now. I really do.

La Passeggiata

Today, you and I are going on a nice walk together, and I will explain to you everything I see.

First of all, you must realize that on the east coast of Sicily, where I live, there is this huge bump in the ground called Mt. Erna, and as a result finding a stretch of land that is horizontal as opposed to vertical is a chore in and of itself.

Nonetheless, I have found an excellent walking course, one that will allow us to experience many different sights, sounds, and colors as we walk our way to good health.

Finding a parking space is always a problem in Aci Castello, that beautiful coastal town on the water that has had an ancient Norman castle protecting it for over a thousand years.

I know the perfect place to park…and what's more, there isn't a blue line on the parking space indicating that we have to pay. Today, we park for free!

Getting out of the car, we put our IPODS on. We need something zippy to listen to…something that gets the blood flowing.

We approach the sweeping vista view of the Ionian Sea just 100 yards away from the castle. Here is where we will stretch a bit, inhale that wonderful sea breeze coming off that glimmering sheen of gold in the water, and gently move our muscles.

The sun, not yet hot or humid is warm. Thank God we walk in the morning as by mid-afternoon the temperature is far too unhealthy to exercise. No, now is the perfect time.

Above us, the Norman Castle, in all its splendor, looms. Looking down into the sea, we notice that it is surrounded by huge boulders…probably placed there centuries ago to protect against invaders. Today we see people in bathing suits lounging on the rocks, with not a care in the world.

Slowly we build up a decent walking pace. We pass a wedding party… someone is getting married today. Let's get closer!

As we approach the bride and groom and their wedding party…we notice they are foreigners…Chinese…who have traveled thousands of miles

142

to marry in this most romantic of spots.

The groom looks dapper...not more than twenty five years old; he is wearing a black shark-skin suit and a red carnation. I notice that he is very handsome.

His bride is wearing perhaps the finest silk wedding gown that I have ever seen. Two precious little girls hold up the train of the gown followed by the four proud parents and a scattering of friends.

They have traveled far for this day, indeed.

We walk a little further now, past the castle and the sea is to our left. We follow the sea on the sidewalk, and appreciate the many vista views we encounter along the way.

Just about everything is in bloom right now; the wild flowers paint the way in an explosion of yellows, reds, pinks, oranges....and the fragrance of the flowers fill your nostrils in a such a way that it leaves an indelible mark on your conscience.

The view as we walk, the explosion on color all around, the sweet spring fragrance of La Sicilia in bloom has a healing affect on the both of us.

Our aches and pains brought across the sea from a harsh New England winter melt away, and the spring in our step tells us that we are healing.

We see others on their walk this morning. Many people want to get in shape for the summer. Young and old walk, jog, run by us. Some greet us with a smile. Others are lost in their own world.

This is their time to relax, contemplate.

We make a big loop now, and we cross the street away from the sea.

Pretty soon we are walking through the tiny streets of Aci Castello and see the town spring to life.

Over on the right, the fish store is opening and the shopkeeper is arranging his wares.

Wow! Looks like he has sword fish on sale today. The sweet smell of the "panificio"...the bread maker... fills the air as the first of the morning bread is coming out of the oven.

Nearby, the green grocer is arranging the fruit in his stand...cherries, peaches, apricots, strawberries...join the tomatoes, broccoli, lettuce mushrooms and onions that overflow on his cart.

We walk past the espresso bar...called simply a "bar" in Sicily and smell the freshly brewed espresso as townspeople sit and enjoy an espresso with a *brioche*...that sweet tasting morning bread that is a staple here. We are getting hungry.

We walk past the old-timers...congregating about the corner and deep in conversation as they solve the world's problems...almost done our walk now...we can see the car from here.

Slowly we finish our walk and begin to cool down. We have worked up a sweat and the cool water we drink satisfies the thirst.

Taking one last look at the shimmering sea, we say to ourselves, "See you tomorrow!"

Now, that is a healthy walk indeed!

Acitrezza on my daily walk from Aci Castello.

The Hunter

Despite my best efforts to seal off every nook and cranny of my house, the mosquitoes of Acitrezza are fully capable of evading even the stingiest of defenses that I can construct and relish their talent of dive bombing right by my ear...usually at 4 AM every morning.

Last week I had screens installed on all the windows of my house, as I remembered very well the welts that accumulated last year on my wrists, forearms and ankles...everyplace that is exposed even for two minutes each night. Draping blankets over my head is an exercise of futility I have found. It must be some sort of advertisement for them, actually.

"Look, there is an American with a blanket over his head." They must say. "I am in the mood for American food tonight. How about you?"

Well, after years of being pushed around helplessly by these little critters, this Sicilian-Ninja decided to strike back.

"Never get a Sicilian mad" I mused. "Now, you will pay."

The first order of business, I decided was to develop an effective swatting technique.

All the usual implements of mosquito death and destruction were tested by this Ninja, including a newspaper, a slipper, a fly swatter and an old towel. I remembered that in my younger days that I could snap a towel with breathtaking efficiency, so that old technique was evaluated.

"Reflexes are gone" I mused. "Snapping won't work," I thought.

I decided on the slipper method. It was light yet deadly. I have used this method in the past and it compensated for my slow reflexes.

"Ok, Alfred" I said. "That's the weapon of choice."

I then stretched out and meditated. Remembering the relaxation techniques of the ancient Chinese mosquito hunters, especially evoking the spirit of the most famous killer of them all, "One Flu By," I readied myself for battle on what was to be this most epic eve of destruction.

My weapon of choice war: my famous size thirteen bedroom slipper, manufactured by Eddie Bauer and a veteran killer of the famous Maine "No See Ums."

Yup. I had chosen the appropriate weapon.

Now, I must set the trap and be quick like a cat.

Tip-toeing up to the door leading out to the deck, I cracked it open an inch. "Let them think I forgot to close it" I thought. "That will keep their guard down."

Using the element of surprise was always an effective battle technique, I was taught.

One by one, they came in. One by one, I hunted them down and "eliminated" them.

"Splat" went the first once. "Squished" went the second. A devastating backhand got the third. A stealth and never seen before maneuver called the "round house right" got the fourth.

I was in a zone.

Retribution this night was swift and just.

The corpses began to pile up.

As I leaped from bed to bureau, from closet top to hamper, I was a Ninja killing machine that night.

The story of legends.

Finally, it ended. The devastation was over, complete, final.

Disposing quickly my implements of destruction and Windexing all the spots on the wall caused by my slipper, I slipped into bed an exhausted but satisfied victor.

Of course, less than two minutes later, an annoying mosquito buzz was heard as one zipped by my ear again.

Not to worry. Tomorrow night the battle will continue. Didn't Troy take ten years to fall to the Greeks? I am a patient man.

I will buy some mosquito netting for the bed tomorrow morning though.

I bet that will help a lot.

I hope.

This past May, I decided that enough was enough.

I was going to get my act together physically because at the rate I was burning the candle, there wasn't much wick left.

The first thing to go was the butts. I had this terrible smoking habit for years. As I was getting older, I knew that smoking just wasn't a good thing. Like any addiction, the mind had to decide first, then the body follows suit.

My mind was easy to convince.

That happened the day my doctor told me that I *MAY* have suffered a heart attack a while ago, and never even noticed it.

Pointing to the pack of cigarettes in my pocket, he said to me "Smoking causes 50% of all heart disease. Isn't it time you stopped being an idiot?"

He was right.

I remember throwing that last pack of butts in his basket as I left the office. That was it for smoking. I bought some toothpicks, and every time I needed to put something in my mouth, I reached for a "stecchino" as they are called in Italian.

The tricky part was not gaining weight. Many of my friends ballooned up after quitting, and at my already bloated size, that was the last thing I wanted.

No, that wasn't happening to me.

I decided to not only stop smoking, but also to start exercising, and lose weight.

The first thing I did was buy a book. Actually, I bought a couple of books on diet and nutrition.

With my personal condition, I had to do three main things: lower my cholesterol, reduce the intake of fat in my diet and really limit the use of salt.

To my horror, when I started looking at the labels in my food pantry, virtually everything in my fridge and cupboards had a lot of sodium in it. I couldn't believe how much sodium things had…especially so since I needed only 1300 mg a day to operate safely.

Eating just a couple of things …like chips…popcorn…maybe soup in a can...and there goes the daily allotment!

Using only 1300 mg of a salt a day required a BIG overhaul on things I loved and I was forced to eliminate a lot of them.

Oh well. What next?

Well, now that you asked, I needed to get the cholesterol under control...and fast.

Sadly, that meant eliminating almost all red meat. No more salami (also packed with salt!), cold cuts in general, steak, lamb...hamburger... just about everything on my weekly shopping list!

Out they went.

In my diet came chicken, fish, grilled veggies, fruit and out went the butter, sour cream and anything else that was high in cholesterol.

Oh well, what next?

Well, now I had to keep track of my fat intake. Just because things don't have cholesterol doesn't automatically mean that you can shovel what's left in your mouth.

Nope. Read the labels.

Shockingly, my all time favorite product...olive oil...had fat. I had the mistaken impression that olive oil was perfectly fine for you...after all it had the "good" cholesterol in it, doesn't it? Well, yes and no. That in and of itself doesn't give you carte blanche to guzzle all the olive oil you want.

The reason? While olive oil it has the "good "cholesterol, it has fat. How much is a good amount to have then? Well, the answer is...three tablespoons a day.

Really a chintzy amount, if you think about it. There goes the bread dipping, for sure.

Actually, I quickly learned the benefits of balsamic vinegar, apple cider vinegar, red wine vinegar, lemon juice, herbs, spices...all your allies...and all helped to stretch that chintzy three tablespoon allotment nicely every single day.

I also switched to skim milk and generally began reading all the labels that I found.

With this in mind, I left for Sicily.

Not only had I stopped smoking, now I was re-learning proper nutrition at my old age, plus I needed to start some sort of an exercise program while I was over there too.

Let's talk about what I ate while in Sicily.

Simple.

I ate pasta three times a week. Exactly 100 grams per sserving. With two tablespoons of olive oil, a whole piece of garlic and black pepper. It satisfied me.

Believe me, it was great. I also ate the pasta at 2 PM every day...that is when I have my "big" meal...just like all Sicilians.

Since pasta is a carbohydrate, I did not have any bread with it. Just a nice salad. And believe me...in Sicily, salads are GREAT! Tomatoes taste like tomatoes...if you know what I mean.

Pizza? Yup. Twice a week. One minor adjustment, that's all.

First of all, very little cheese. Yes, that is correct. Very little cheese. Too much fat and cholesterol. I eliminated almost all the cheese from my pizza. Instead, I ask for the vegetarian with GRILLED vegetables and just a DRIZZLE of oil.

Believe me, that super-thin crust loaded with grilled veggies (tomatoes, eggplant, zucchini, mushrooms, onions) was simply heaven.

Usually, these pizza are much smaller in size than the American version, so two slices were great...along with a salad.

How about protein? Don't you need protein? Sure...I will give you a bunch of choices, but here are my two favorites.

First, I went to the supermarket and but a half kilo of *"pesce spada"* (sword fish) cut no more than a quarter inch to a half inch thick.

Then I make a mixture of fresh parsley, olive oil (one tablespoon, black pepper, and lemon juice). This is my marinade.

The secret is to have a good grilling pan.

A grilling pan is a flat pan sold all over the place. It has ridges on it to drip away the fat. The secret here is to get that pan HOT. On a medium high gas stove, place that grilling pan. I get a paper towel and LIGHTLY rub some olive oil on it...really a negligible amount.

Then, I put my marinade on one side of the sword fish and lay it on the pan. While it is cooking, I lay my veggies on the pan too. Let those suckers cook. After exactly four minutes, flip the sword fish and turn the veggies. Four minutes after that, you have the perfect meal. Grilled sword fish and grilled veggies (any veggies will do…I like asparagus, mushroom, zucchini…anything really).

Chicken is a great substitute with that exact same marinade.

Chicken or fish…many variants of fish beside sword fish…tuna…white fish…you name it… and also chicken thighs…breasts…(without the skin) and you are in business.

Twice a week, I rewarded myself with a *granita* and *brioche* for breakfast too!

Breakfast? I would have low fat cereal, or whole wheat toast or oatmeal…with decaf coffee (o.k. admit…half decaf, half regular)…the breakfast of champions.

Of course, there were a million other things I tried, but these worked for me…and I am one happy camper.

The only thing left: Exercise. Exercising in Sicily is a piece of cake.

Provided you find a flat stretch of lane to walk or jog.

I walked every day along the ocean road from Acitrezza to Aci Castello…a sweeping vista overlook the majestic Ionian Sea, and believe me, that one hour walk that I did zipped right by. I have 28 tunes that I downloaded on my IPOD…and when I listened to all of them…my walk was finished…exactly one hour.

Finally: stress management. Here is what I decided…honestly.

Screw the bills.

What is the worst that could happen?

My credit gets ruined? So what? I decided to live every day as it is my last, not for my credit score. Besides, I have never seen a *U Haul It* behind a hearse on the way to the cemetery, have you?

The banks have pulled the biggest heist in human history with credit cards, and I for one have walked away from them and the rat race.

Honestly, it wasn't a hard decision.

In any case, this is the direction I am headed…and I feel a lot better now that I have the rudiments of a plan to stick with.

Then again, plans can be changed, but for now, I am focused, happy, and loving every minute!

If I wanted to write about beautiful, historical, cultural and unforgettable places to see, I think the only words I would write about Sicily is this: **SEE ANYPLACE IN SICILY. YOU WILL FORGET NOTHING.**

That said, in my last book "*The Reverse Immigrant*," I wrote about several places that I enjoyed, and this time I decided to do the same.

For those of you who have never been to Sicily, words (especially by me) are not sufficient. You should experience these places.

There is plenty online material now … You-Tube material…Facebook material…and the amount is growing by leaps and bounds every month… to give even the more curious lover of Sicily many hours of enjoyment.

In no particular order, the following places are SOME of my favorites and if you were with me, I would take you there.

A. *Palermo: The Sanctuary Of Santa Rosalia*

You have no idea how fervent people in Palermo are about Santa Rosalia. July 13th to 15th every year is the celebration in Palermo…and Sicily's biggest city comes to a screeching halt then.

The story is well known: She came from nobility but her father was caught up in a plot against the royal family. He was killed and the family fortune confiscated.

Rosalia turned to Jesus and lived in a cave on Monte Pellegrino for nearly five years until her death in September of 1166 AD.

Four hundred and fifty years later, in 1625, a devastating plague hit the city brought on by diseased animals from arriving ships.

By now she was a venerated woman…someone who had given her life to Jesus. In any case, her relics were carried through the streets of Palermo and the scourge of the plague ended immediately.

In a cave where she lived on Mount Pellegrino is her shrine.

There, you will find the breath-taking statue of Santa Rosalia…solid gold…donated by King Charles III long ago…along with many pieces of jewelry donated over the centuries by the faithful…and you will be awed.

My friend Manfredi Barbera took me there for the first time many years ago. I remember the feeling of overwhelming spirituality the first time I visited the cave.

I have returned many times over the years, and this place is near the top of my personal list.

B. *Palermo: Teatro Massino*

You probably have seen the inside of this beautiful opera house if you saw the last movie of the Godfather Trilogy.

The opera scenes were shot here.

Then again, so was Michael Corleone's daughter…right on the steps.

That said, this building is known for much more than a movie being filmed there.

Completed almost at the beginning of the twentieth century, some of Italy's most famous artists and sculptors contributed their talents to its construction, and the result of their labor was Europe's largest opera house …both in size… and in capacity.

Patrons flock to the Teatro Massimo for the most important cultural events and the national Italian television stations extensively broadcast many concerts, plays, operas and art events from this venue.

The acoustics, it is said, are spectacular.

While Catania has its own version of a beautiful theater, really, this is the one to check out if you are an art aficionado.

C. *Palermo: The Royal Palace and Palentine Chapel*

There are so many beautiful chapels, cathedrals, churches, basilicas and sanctuaries in Sicily… To pick out just a single place that is the *MOST* beautiful is an exercise in futility.

However, both the Royal Palace and Palatine Chapel needs to be visited by you before you make your own decision as which is the most beautiful in Sicily. This visit needs to be made and be part of your consideration.

If this book was a pretty picture book, I would be able to show you all the breathtaking nooks and crannies of both places…however…this book is not a pretty book BUT you can take on the internet a virtual tour right after reading this article by simply Googling "The Palatine Chapel." See what comes up. Sit back and enjoy!

The Palatine Chapel or Monreale Chapel?

For me, they are "too close to call." I rank them numbers 1 and number 1A.

As famous writers have written, the Palentine Chapel is perhaps one of the finest chapels *EVER* built.

During its heyday, it was the seat of great cultural accomplishments.

For example, in Roger's Room in the Palace...where the great Fredrick II assembled the greatest literary writers of his age...the Sicilian School of Poetry was born.

The first poems in ITALIAN, according to legend, were written here.

Today, the Palace is the seat of the Regional Sicilian Government and the entire complex is breathtaking to view.

Put these two on your list of "must sees" when you come to Sicily.

You will not regret it.

D. *Tindari: The Madonna of Tindari*

Some people refer to her as The Black Madonna, but this sanctuary in a town just west of Messina on the coast is worth the trip.

The sanctuary itself is not one of the best cathedrals that I have seen, truth be told. It was built in the middle of the sixteenth century as a matter of fact. Practically new by Sicilian standards.

However, the Black Madonna, which is a Byzantine/style wooden statue, is the story here. The statue will humble you.

You will feel the presence of the mother of Jesus in this church. I did.

Tindari is located just off the autostrada as you travel west from Messina west. The exit sign is clearly marked. It is easy to find.

The day that we went was a clear and sunny day.

I went there to pick up a replica of the statue for a friend of mine and on the way there read up about it and its history.

We attended Mass and later enjoyed ourselves as we visited many religious stands operated by the nuns, who were very savvy, by the way, in the art of business negotiation.

To folks in this part of Sicily, this is one very special place, and I agree totally with their feelings.

This is a holy place.

The vara of Santa Rosalie...simply magnificent.

Since my first visit, I have returned three times to this wonderful place. I am happy each time I visit there, too.

E. *Agrigento: The Valley of the Temples*

If you visit nothing else in Sicily, then Agrigento and the Valley of the Temples needs to be near the top of your list.

The city of Agrigento itself has a history that goes back five centuries BC to the days of the Greek tyrants, the conflict with Carthage, and later the Roman era.

This place is one huge museum and should be studied a bit before visiting.

You will be surprised by the size, quality, and condition of the wonderful Greek ruins too.

At nighttime, several of them have specially installed lighting that is breathtaking to behold.

The Temple Of Hera Lacina, The Temple of Herakles, The Temple of Hera and Paestum merely scratch the surface here. There is a lot to see in this area.

The area also features the wonderful Regional Archaeological Museum in San Nicola, reputed to be Sicily's best.

This area will tie things together for you and put Sicily in wonderful historical perspective.

Thanks to the internet and the wonder of search engines, most of the places that I mentioned in this chapter have virtual online tours available for you.

As I mentioned above, there are literally hundreds of places that will inspire you and these places that I mentioned are a representative sampling of Ancient Sicily.

Sicilia Bedda.

The Trinacria, ancient symbol of Sicily.

Yes, there is a dark side in Sicily and you should be aware of it. Exploitation of middle aged women.

Like any country Sicily has things that seem unfair, unjust and just plain wrong. However, as a Sicilian-American that had the very best that America has to offer in terms of upbringing, profession, education and opportunity, some things stick out like a sore thumb today, and I want to write about it and expose it.

A very close friend of mine is a woman aged 44 years. She is intelligent, hard working, honest, dependable, bi-lingual, and ethical. She has been out of work now for over a year.

She lives a hand to mouth existence. Since she is single and unemployed, she hasn't the safety net of unemployment insurance that we have in the states.

Every day, she is on the computer searching for a job. Faithfully and with great discipline she responds to any conceivable ad that may be a potential fit.

Most, however, respond in this way: "Sorry, you are too old."
Huh?

Too old at 44 years of age? Isn't that illegal? Isn't that discrimination? Can't they get into trouble for saying that to a prospective employee?
Well, no.

Unlike America which has very strong laws in terms of discrimination based on a whole series of issues, sex, age, gender, handicap, religion, etc., in Italy, while some of those things are technically "on the books", employers are pretty much free to do as they please.

One time she called me excited because a prospective employer was possibly interested in hiring her. She had sent them her resume, a cover letter, and followed up with a phone call several days later.

They emailed her and asked her to send them a full length photo of her. Not a head shot photo...a full length photo!

Huh? Isn't that illegal? Can an employer request a full profile photo? Isn't that discrimination, sexual harassment...something?

The most promising offer of all, however, was a school that was looking for a bi-lingual (English and Italian) translator and instructor to teach biology courses, write chapters in books on biology, and to translate letters from Italian into English.

I remember that day well.

The interview was on the other side of Catania and she asked me for a ride to the prospective employer as she didn't want to be late taking a bus.

On the way to Catania I tried to give her advice the best I could. I told her to be confident, look the prospective employer in the eyes when talking, give him a firm handshake, and to remain calm and focused on his questions.

She listened to every word I said.

I dropped her at the appointed place and waited for her, hoping that things would go well. If anyone in Sicily needed a break in life, this was the woman. Without this job, she would be homeless by month's end, and most importantly, her spirit would be crushed.

As I waited, I decided that I was as nervous as she was. I silently said a prayer to God, asking for his intercession.

One hour later, my cell phone rang. "Alfred" she said, "They like me. They want me to take a biology test in English that will take an hour. Can you wait a little while longer?"

After assuring her that I wasn't going anywhere except waiting for her, I waited.

And waited.

Another two hours passed.

Finally, I saw her.

"I took the test and received a perfect score of 100%" she said. "The director told me that in five days he will think about an offer and call me."

She was elated. Could this be the break that she needed?

Five days passed and to tell you the truth, I was as nervous as she.

We talked about the minimum amount of money she could possibly accept. We worked on a budget to see how much money she would need to survive as a single woman in Catania.

One room places in Catania to rent were 450 euro a month.

Then she had to eat, buy clothes for work, pay for gasoline for her scooter, pay for her cell phone.

We calculated that an offer of 1200 euro a month would enable her to accomplish these things, plus maybe even save a few euro too. That worked out to $1,680 US dollars a month...about $420 a week...roughly $22,000 USD a year for a forty four year old woman to survive in a big city...not exactly opulent, but at least it was a start.

The next day, the offer came.

Here is what the offer was: Six day work week, ten hours per day. Total per week: sixty hours. Monthly pay: 600 euro (that is 150 euro a week). That works out to $840 USD a months or $210 USD a week. Divided by a sixty hour work week, that amounted to $3.50 USD per hour!

Disgraceful.

My stomach twisted when I heard that offer. I knew what the employer was thinking: "She's old, she is out of work, and she is desperate. She will take this job and I will benefit."

Looking at me with eyes that spoke volumes, She was devastated. I said to her "We'll keep looking. I will help you, don't worry."

When I went home, I finally understood why millions of the best and brightest had left Sicily over the last one hundred years.

Exploitation.

Pure and simple.

Multiply this story a hundred thousand times and you will begin to understand the agony that Sicilian people have endured.

This must stop. The famous American jurist Justice Brandies once said: "Sunlight is the best disinfectant." Today, I am disinfecting by relating this story.

Perhaps, in my own way, I can shed light on what the best and brightest minds in Sicily must endure...in this day and age.

To finish the story: I made calls when I returned home to America and secured a job for her here. She is thinking about accepting it. Another Sicilian thinking about leaving Sicily.

Then again, she has to eat, doesn't she?

Postscript: Shortly after I returned to America, I received an email from her. She accepted a sixty-hour per week position as a snack bar worker in a local prison. Her pay? About five dollars per hour. As she says, "Better than nothing."

The Sicilian Flag, the Trinacria, the Carretto, and Pupi Siciliani

Before I start discussing the Sicilian flag, the Trinacria, the carretto, and the pupi Siciliani, I need to tell you about Professor Gaetano Cipolla and this wonderful organization Arba Sicula.

He is the man that you turn to in order to learn about Sicily. He is the master.

Professor Cipolla has spent his entire academic life in the research of anything pertaining to Sicily…its culture, language, history, poetry, prose, and art.

He has a voluminous knowledge of just about every facet of Sicilian lore and legend too.

If my book that you are reading today motivates you in any way to research Sicily, I suggest you start with the body of work Professor Cipolla has assembled. My little piece below should serve merely to whet the appetite.

I joined his organization Arba Sicula years ago, and I recommend that you do also.

On the website is www.arbasicula.org. You can read about Sicily and her culture and support its mission by purchasing many books that he and others have authored on the subject.

His site has long been one of my favorites.

That said, I can further say this about Professor Gaetano Cipolla: his work on Sicily hasn't been the result of a professional endeavor…rather, it has been his vocation, his calling.

Truly, this man's vocation in life has been to educate Americans AND Sicilians on Sicily.

He is not only a son of Sicily, but also her most brilliant intellect since World War II.

I truly admire and respect the man.

Professor Cipolla was born in Francavilla di Sicilia (ME) and studied in Catania before he came to America. He knows the city well and he is fan of the Catania soccer team like myself. We, therefore, have another thing in common, besides our love of Sicily.

Professor Cipolla told me once that the colors of the Sicilian flag come from the colors of Spain-Aragonese flags. This is my view too. However, there are other beliefs in the flag's origins too.

Another version popular in Palermo is that the color red comes from Palermo (as the color red has stood for many years as its "color") and the color gold comes from Corleone (its color).

Both areas were stalwarts in the Sicilian Vespers uprising which eventually drove the French from Sicily. In those days, by the way, Corleone had nothing to do with Francis Ford Coppola and the Godfather Trilogy. Rather was one of the biggest agricultural centers in the region and this theory certainly has merit.

Still others prefer the story that the color red symbolizes the fire of Etna and the color gold the sun. The tourism industry certainly promotes Sicily as the "Isola del Sole"…Island of the Sun.

What everyone CAN agree on, however, is who is in the image in the center.

That one is easy.

That is the Gorgon named Medusa.

Greek mythology tells us that she was beheaded by the hero Perseus who was sent by the king to cut off her head as a gift to himself. Perseus cleverly used his shield's reflection to see her, thus avoiding directly looking at her and getting himself turned into stone, and was able to kill her and cut off her head.

After turning a bunch of his enemies into stone himself by flashing her head at them (including the king who ordered him to go on this adventure in the first place), he ended up giving the head to the Greek goddess Athena…who wore its image on all her armor as protection. Statues of Athena have this image on her breast plate or cape to this day.

The rest of the symbol…wheat…surrounding Medusa's head… symbolizes the island's fertility…and then we have those famous three legs pointing in three different directions.

What's the story with the legs?

Well, it depends who you ask.

There are hundreds and hundreds of myths about the origins of those legs, but one thing I do know is that many of these myths go back a long time...back to the Greek mythology period.

One story was that the major god Zeus once got annoyed at three nymphs who would go to ancient Sicily and take things and throw them into the sea just for fun. He stood them upside down to hold up the island and look for those things as a puniishment.

Another story that I know about is that the ancient name of Sicily, Trinakrais means "triangle" and her great cities evolved from its name.

My preferred story is that the legs point to the three areas that her people come from North (Europe), South (North Africa), and East (Greece).

Still others say that they point to her great cities of Palermo, Siracusa and Messina.

In any case, there are hundreds more. These are but a few.

What IS accurate though is that the flag has been in official use since January, 2000 and is know flown over all official buildings in Sicily.

Today, the Sicilian flag is a source of unity and pride to all Sicilians.

It has become the rallying point for Sicilians to maintain their own cultural identity...much to the consternation of a lot of people...regular Italians included.

Here is what I know: The symbol of Sicily and her origins span thousands of years. Not hundreds of years, rather thousands of years.

The ground that I walk on in Sicily has been walked on by many previous scores of generations of people from literally all over the place. Perhaps it was founded by the refugees from Troy who were looking for a place to live after its fall, according to legend. Who knows?

In any case, the symbol of the trinicria and now her flag are very important to me...and to a lot of other folks, too.

Carretto

Another interesting but more recent cultural symbol is that of the Sicilian cart and driver...we call them "carretto." The term "carrettino," is used for the miniature carts you bring home as souvenirs.

Replicas are sold at every tourist shop in Sicily and they range in price from a few euro to many thousands of euro.

In my career, I have dealt with both of the price spectrums and price.

The back of a Sicilian cart made by Salvatore Chiarrenza of Aci Reale. He was one of Sicily's master cart makers.

The cart originally was designed to be pulled by a donkey or a horse for light loads…as much as one animal can pull actually.

They were found originally simple work vehicles used by the Sicilian farmer who used them for his livehood in the fields and to deliver his crops to the market.

Over time, these carts were used to take part in religious festivals held in every town, and skilled woodworkers, artisans, painters and metal workers began to make carts more for artistic purposes rather than for utilitarian purposes.

Painters usually painted depictions of the Normans vanquishing the Saracens on the side panels or perhaps of a Spanish scene (I recently saw one depicting Columbus' voyage), or a religious collage, but the depictions of the Normans are the most prevalent.

If you ever listened to the seminal and most famous Sicilian opera by Pietro Mascagni "Cavalleria Rusticana," based on the on the short story and play by the Sicilian Giovanni Verga (from a prominent family from Catania by the way), one of the central characters, Alfio, was a driver of a *carretto* who made a pretty good living…however, his wife cheated on him with Turiddu and Alfio later killed him in a showdown.

I bet you are familiar with this opera…this was the opera that Michael Corleone's son was singing in *Godfather III*.

In any case, the *carretto* became a symbol of the Sicilian peasant.

Back in the year 2001, when I was involved with my company All Things Sicilian, I found the best *carretto* restorer on the island, a man named Salvatore Chiarenza in Acireale and brought one from him to bring to America. For years we displayed it and eventually we sold it to John Russo in Grand Rapids, Michigan who has a very big retail operation there for Sicilian and Italian wines and foods.

To me, the highlight of my year comes every May 10th when I attend the Feast of Saint Alfio in Trecastagni and watch the parade of the carretini before the Mass. There, about fifty *carretti*…pulled by horses in all their resplendent glory…with their gaily colored plumes and pulling men and boys in their carts playing Sicilian folk music…is the highlight of my pilgrimage.

Pupi Siciliani

Sicilian puppets or "pupi siciliani" are known the world over.

If you have never seen one, do not think that they are the type of puppet that you put over your hand. They are not. Rather, they are elaborate creations with moving parts…arms, legs, and head…controlled by strings with the help of a puppeteer.

Since the Sicilian word is somewhat misleading, I think the French word "marionette" is more appropriate.

In any case, whatever you call them; they too are an important piece of Sicilian cultural history to ignore and today are an important source of income for those who cater to the tourist's trade.

These puppets usually range in price (again) from ten or fifteen euros to thousands of euros.

They are made of medal, cloth, and are hand painted. Different areas of Sicily have different versions of the puppets, but Palermo, Messina, and Catania support many families who have made these pupi for generations. There are many puppet theaters around greater Palermo, Messina and Catania today that stage wonderful shows for children and adults.

As a matter of fact, if you are ever in the Palermo area, the Cuticchio

This cart was brought in by us years ago, and is not proudly on display at my friend John Russo's Wine and Deli in Grand Rapids, Michigan. A truly spectacular piece.

Puppet Theatre and the Pasqualino Marionette Museum are two interesting stops for you. I think they are Sicily's best.

My favorite puppi (there are several variants here) are those that depict the Normans battling the Saracens.

Figures such as Orlando, Rinaldo, Carlo Magno and the Saracen are all popular puppets. Collectors buy and sell the most expensive.

Life size puppets, which I have seen, can cost thousands of euros. Although the bigger ones are not used by the puppet theaters, hotels and restaurants the world over import these items as part of their hotel décor, and collectors now buy and sell them on EBAY too!

While there are possibly hundreds of different types of "symbols" of Sicily that you can learn about, I have presented for you the most rudimentary of them in the hopes that something will strike your fancy and compel you to do further research on the subject.

Whether it is researching the origin of the Trinacria, the flag, the Sicilian carts or the Sicilian puppets...you have to admit it is a lot of fun to learn about these things!

The Treasured Old Guard: Never Forgotten

I am going to introduce you to people that you never met in your life but I thiink that you know very well.

I'd like to introduce you to Scappy and Madeline.

Scappy is the hero father who worked his fingers to the bone in order to give his family a chance at a better life, and Madeline is his daughter who learned the lessons of the father well, became a a full-fledged daughter of Sicily, and has now passed her love of Sicily on to her children.

You see, every family has a Scappy and Madeline...maybe with different names, that's all.

I think you will like their story. I bet it is remarkably similar to someone you know.

Back when I was a young boy many years ago, my extended family was large, young and very close.

Not only were mom and dad still alive, but also my grandparents, my aunts, my uncles, and all my cousins.

The clan was a large and vibrant one.

As the years passed and we got older, those in the "old guard" began to age and pass on.

Try as we may, we were never able to reverse the passage of time, and one by one we said our goodbyes to our loved ones as they embraced the Good Lord's bosom.

What never aged though...was their memory in our mind's eye.

I remember each loved one now as if they are here today with me... in the prime of their life, fit as a fiddle.

It is within this frame of reference that I can tell you now about Scappy and Madeline ...people that impacted me first five decades ago...... who faded away into my memory ...only to come roaring back recently.

Here is their (my) story and the lessons learned from this story perhaps you will take to your heart. I know I did.

Uncle Scappy

Prelude:

About a month ago, I got an email from my cousin Joe concerning cousin Madeline. Madeline was the daughter of uncle Scappy.

Uncle Scappy had moved to California with his family, and since I infrequently saw them as a young boy, I didn't know them very well. Once a year though Scappy returned to Massachusetts with his family, including Madeline.

Cousin Joe told me that Madeline was planning a trip to Sicily and could I please re-establish contact with her to give her a run down on Sicily…tell her where to go, suggest to her what to see…pretty much the same request that I get from many people who know that I spend a lot of time there.

I agreed and promised Joe that I would re-establish contact. Joe and Madeline are first cousins and are close.

His father "Mimmu," and Madeline's father "Scappy" along with their sisters Lucy and Millie were first cousins with my mom. Not only were Lucy and Millie my mom's first cousins, they were also mom's best friends, and not a single day went by that the "girls" didn't talk.

As I later found out, their mother and mom's mother were sisters who grew up in the same house in Trecastagni…the Gangi House.

Since they were all so close to mom, it was a BIG Deal when Scappy would come to Lawrence to visit from San Jose, California, where he and his family lived.

For a brief time every year, the four siblings, Scappy, Mimmu, Lucy and Millie were re-united, and my family always took time to celebrate their reunion with them.

Mom would always insist upon it. It was a huge event, believe me.

Back in the 1950s, San Jose California was far away. By far away, I mean FAR away. No one from my family EVER went there. It was far away!

Mom would say the word "California" like it was in another galaxy. "San Jose" sounded absolutely foreign.

Thus, when uncle Scappy and his family visited town, it was a very big news indeed.

He and his wife Nellie (Leone), another Sicilian, had moved to San Jose in order to seek a better way of life for their family. San Jose's weather was compelling as opposed to the harsh New England climate.

I remember Scappy being a warm and loving man with a brown wavy hair and a big smile on his face who hugged the hell out of me when he saw me. He always asked me a lot of questions…especially about school.

Even though I saw him infrequently, I loved the guy.

He oozed love.

With uncle Scappy would be his daughter Madeline. She was an extraordinarily smart and beautiful girl five years older than I. She was born in Massachusetts but moved to California when she was two and a half years old. She was tall and lean and had big brown eyes.

Since the visits were only once a year, Madeline grew up without knowing very well our very big extended family. She learned about the family second hand from Scappy. She learned a LOT of things from Scappy, but the family "Back East" was one thing he taught her.

When she did come to Massachusetts, the visits were fairly short and by the time I would get re-acquainted with her, it would be over.

What I remember about Madeline back then was that she was a free spirit…even at a young age, and extraordinarily smart and beautiful. Little else.

Scappy had done well…very well…in San Jose. He made up for his lack of schooling (he had only a sixth grade education) with guts, determination, and hard work.

Uncle Joe "Scappy" Ponti doing what he loved to do best: cook!

Like my grandfather Gaetano Torrisi, Scappy knew the art of using hammer and nail, and as the years passed he went from a blue collar worker to the owner of his own apartment buildings in San Jose.

One thing that Scappy did even better than his professional accomplishments, however, was to install into Madeline a profound love of her Sicilian ancestry.

She was brought up Sicilian, not Italian…as were we all. Only a Sicilian can understand that sentence I guess.

She was raised with the best of values, morals, and taste for the "exceptional" intellectual things in life.

She learned opera…Scappy loved opera. She ate Sicilian cuisine… her mom was Sicilian and an excellent cook, and she was urged to read great literature.

Scappy and Nellie, like their entire generation…sacrificed their lives for their children and tried to give them the very best of everything.

Devotion to his children, absolute love, sacrifice, and hard work were the hallmark of Scappy's life.

He was doing in California with his family exactly what my mom and dad were doing to us in New England: leading a parallel existence a continent apart with the same core values being simultaneously instilled into both families.

As Scappy was busy providing Madeline these core life values, my parents were doing the same thing to us.

As a result, Madeline prospered, graduating from college and attained a graduate degree…the same as my siblings and I, except a continent away.

She settled in Etna, California. (Etna California…ironic name, isn't it?) and has been married to the same man for nearly forty years. (here is where we differ…she did that with one man…it took me several wives to hit that mark!)

When Scappy died in 1992 at the age of 80, it was Madeline who cared for him in her home in Etna, and it was she that closed his eyes when he passed.

Like a good daughter, she comforted him up until the last moment. The pluperfect Sicilian daughter.

Normally the story would end there…a wonderful father who gave his family his all, and who died a peaceful death surrounded by his loved ones. This story was repeated tens of thousands of times by other Sicilians around America, wasn't it?

However, another chapter was unfolding…something quite different, startling…and very romantic too.

Keep reading.

Aftermath:

Madeline raised four beautiful children on her ranch in Northern California as her life moved on after the death of Scappy.

Like Scappy, she did things herself: raised farm animals, sheered the sheep, spun the wool, knitted, cooked, reared the children. Keeping the family ranch running smoothly was no easy task, but the lessons provided by Scappy served her well. Her kids grew, eventually married, and moved away.

However, at age 55…like her father had done before her…she did something out of the ordinary.

Extraordinary, really.

Throwing caution to the wind (just like Scappy had done decades earlier) she and her husband Ken bought a beautiful wooden schooner, Compass Rose, and cruised the east coast for seven years.

Not the west coast…the east coast!

A sixty foot vessel! A sailboat!

They bought a sixty foot sailboat, and for seven years traveled up and down the east coast…after teaching themselves how to sail!

However, the story gets better. In 2009, they purchased a Lord Nelson Victory Tug…a tug boat…in Kusadasi, Turkey and have been cruising the Aegean Sea ever since!

The vessel's name? The boat's name is "Mamma Mia!" in honor of her mother and her Sicilian heritage.

Thus, Madeline had become a wanderer too…straying far from her home in California with her husband…and is the only "mate" on her tug boat in the Aegean Sea!

On her boat, she makes her own flags, does all the rope work and all the cosmetic upkeep on the vessel.

She has become a real "Sicilian Tug Boat Annie!"

Now, comes the good part:

Uncle Scappy's daughter Madeline as a child. Now, she cruises the Aegean Sea with a tugboat! A true daughter of Sicily!

After nearly forty years, we talked last month.

She called me and told me that she planning on visiting Sicily in September. As the conversation progressed, I thought to myself that she and I were remarkably similar and that I had found a kindred spirit with my cousin.

We "friended" each other on Facebook. We now email daily to one another. Her lovely daughter Maria "friended" me too and both read my book *The Reverse Immigrant*.

They not only enjoyed it, but I think it helped re-kindled the flame of love that these daughters of Sicily have for La Sicilia!

In any case, Madeline is moving her tug boat...to a new location hopefully next summer.

Want to take a guess where?

Yup.

The coast of Sicily.

She is looking for a sleepy fishing village somewhere in Sicily to dock her tug right now.

Can you imagine that?

She is the seafaring version of me...a kindred spirit with a longing to return to her ancestral roots.

I wonder what Scappy would say to her now if he were alive.

I know he is looking down at her from heaven and smiling...no... positively beaming...that Madeline has come full circle, and like Scappy before her, placed Sicily firmly right smack dab in the middle of her heart.

What a peach...my cousin Madeline.

A true daughter of Sicily.

Then again, she's Sicilian, isn't she?

The Sicilian Robin Hood?

This past July 5th marked the sixty-first anniversary of the death of Salvatore "Turiddu" Giuliano, still admired by many in Sicily in a Robin Hood sort of way.

Not everyone feels that way about him, however.

Some feel he was a thug, robber, egomaniac, and killer who got his just desserts.

Every time I talk with someone from the greater Palermo area about the goings on in Sicily at the end of the Second War and into 1950, Turiddu Giuliano's name is brought up.

It is impossible to talk about that period without bringing up his name, actually. The thing is this: most of the facts that surround who he was, what he did, who he it did it with and why he did it, are subject to much speculation...and with Sicilians, speculation is a way of life.

More recently, he seems to have become a rallying point of sorts for the nascent Independent Sicily Movement that has sprung up in parts of America (New York City) and in parts of Sicily (areas immediately around both the universities of Palermo and Catania frequented by left leaning students and academics).

The Movement for an Independent Sicily isn't a recent contrivance by these people...Turiddu Giuliano fought under the banner of Sicilian independence...at least initially, anyway.

I find it odd that the left (almost anyone associated with an independent Sicily movement today is left of center) has embraced Turiddu the way it has of late, because immediately after the war he advocated strongly for Sicily becoming a state in the USA, and legend has it that he even wrote President Truman a letter back then suggesting this idea.

He also (at least initially) fought both the socialists and the mafia with his band of merry machine-gun toting men.

His charming good looks and penchant for publicity quickly made him a favorite with the down trodden in the western part of the island. Within a matter of time however, he had gone global thanks to the Italian and international press.

I am sure that if he were alive today, he would be using all the social media…Facebook, Twitter, My Space…to promote his cause, because in that respect (promoting himself) he was way ahead of the curve.

By 1950, however, his run at fame was dimming and he was on the run…having been blamed for leading an attack that allegedly killed thirteen innocent civilians and wounded scores of others.

His star had been waning for some time before that incident actually, as he and his band of followers had resorted to kidnappings, robbery and banditry as a cash crop way of financing their objectives.

His whole story is rife with intrigue as far as I can see.

Those who supported him back then (and to this day) say that the Italian government and/or the mafia set him up.

His supporters still say that he ordered his men to fire over the heads of the victims and that mafia killers were the culprits. They say that the Italian govenmnet orchestrated the whole thing.

It makes no difference.

By 1950 he was killed and buried.

Then again, was he?

Official stories that came out about his death say that he was shot by a policeman (carabiniere) sent there to track him down.

His backers say it was one of his own men who set him up under a deal with the government only to himself be poisoned four years later.

Others say that he wasn't killed at all…that he fled to the USA. Rumor has it that the authorities dug up his body last year to examine his DNA. Who knows the truth?

The rumors persist, the legend continues to grow.

Mario Puzo wrote a book based on him called *The Sicilian*, and Hollywood made a movie about him too. Plays have been written, ballads, and every day someone online seems to sing his praises.

Why?

Well, for some, he represented (or represents) the thought of a free Sicily…a Sicily governed by Sicilians. After all, he flew the Sicilian Independence Flag (it looks like an American flag except there the stars were replaced by the trinacria).

The Free Sicily movement never gained traction back then, and frankly won't today either. When Sicilians actually voted on the issue back then, those supporting independence revived only single digit support.

The again, his supporters say that the vote was rigged.

(Sigh)

We'll never know the truth I have concluded.

His profoundly good looks…movie star good looks actually, his leadership skills, and his tactual victories made him legend and now have spawned a cottage industry for those who wish on a star for a free Sicily.

My take is simple: *IF* the Italian government someday decides to give Sicily its independence (believe me, that day will never come…far too many Italian politicians make far too much money the way the system works presently) and *IF* someone comes up with a solution to the "mafia" problem in Sicily, then *MAYBE* I will think about it again.

The brutal reality is this: the "mafia" culture and the "national Italian" culture…now deeply ingrained in the consciousness of the people…will never let this happen.

However inspirational and wonderful the idea of an independent Sicily is to some, unless they *FIRST* come up with a solution to the mafia problem, they will not be taken seriously by anyone, because ten minutes after the government leaves, the mafia would be calling the shots in Sicily…and that is the grim reality, unfortunately.

I like Turiddu Giuliano…at least I like the mystical persona of the guy. I like the whole idea of the handsome Sicilian hero fighting for the oppressed and vanquishing the villains.

Way back then…post World War II…he captured the imagination of desperate and starving Sicilians as they cleared the ruble of the Allied bombings from their destroyed cities and towns only to see the criminals of the mafia take the reconstruction of Sicily and become rich themselves.

They understood as the years passed on and the First mafia war broke out and then the Second mafia war broke out and as the upwards of 10,000 were killed in these mafias wars in the following decades…police, judges, civilians…that the idea of a figure of justice…a hero…a savior of the Sicilian people…was needed.

I do not think that Turiddu Giuliano is that guy though. I think the truth likes somewhere in the middle.

I think that by the time he was killed on July 5, 1950, he was in cahoots with everyone worth getting into cahoots with; because that's the way it was back then.

Back then?

Isn't it the same way today?

Well, yes.

However, Turiddu Giuliano will live on in history, as the economy worsens in Sicily, as more and more youngsters get disillusioned with the way things are there, the the idea of an independent Sicily will be re-visited again and again.

No matter how you feel about Turiddu, he is an interesting and colorful character from Sicily's not so distant past.

My next door neighbor in Acitrezza, Mrs. Longo is one cool dudette. She is senior citizen with a whimsical way of dealing with life.

More than one time in the past she has caught me doing dumb things, but she never gets annoyed at me, mad at me or says anything mean to me.

Most of the time, actually, it seems that she likes the dumb things that I do. Last year she caught me dancing in my boxer shorts while listening to my IPOD on my back deck. She ended up dancing with me.

She is the typical Sicilian senior citizen…she always wears a black frock and she always seems to have a black sweater on…even in the hottest weather…she always wears slippers around the house and yard…and she wears her nylons knotted at the knees. She is a little thing too, barely breaking five feet.

Not only is Mrs. Longo my neighbor in Sicily, but various versions of Mrs. Longo were created and dispersed throughout the world long ago… Boston, New York City, Chicago, Rome, Naples, Palermo…all have versions of Mrs. Longo…because her "look" is the arch-typical "senior Italian lady" look, I think.

In any case, I like my version of Mrs. Longo the best. She probably is a direct decent of the clone version that we have seen everywhere in our lives. As a matter of fact, I bet she is the original clone.

I remember one hot summer day a couple of years ago when the Sicilian sun was simply scorching.

Practically nothing was moving that day.

The searing heat compelled even the most hearty to jump in their car and head to the sea. The beaches were loaded. Even the birds were walking, not wanting to exert energy.

For some reason, heat had no effect on Mrs. Longo.

In the morning on that particular day, I saw her sweeping her deck, dressed in her usual black garb, complete with sweater. Later on that day, she was in the front garden picking rosemary and basil.

Being a little curious as to how Mrs. Longo could operate in such

My grandfather Alfio kept cool in the summer with the exact same recipe a Mrs. Longo...peaches and wine! Of course!

a steaming hot environment unaffected by the heat, my curiosity got the best of me.

In my ridiculously inept version of halting Sicilian I said to her "Buongiorno, signora Longo, pretty hot today, huh?"

"Ciao, Alfredo," she said. "No, I am fine. I won't melt."

"How do you manage to stay cool?" I asked.

"Peaches" she said. "I eat one peach in the morning and another one in the afternoon."

Hmm... peaches. Must be a Sicilian remedy for beating the heat, I thought. Maybe I should try it.

The next time I went to the market, I bought peaches.

Two days later, that scorching heat returned. I had left the peaches in my fruit bowl to ripen a bit. I wanted them nice and juicy.

I ate the first one. Delicious. Later in the day, I ate the second one. Yummy.

However, I was still hot as hell. The peaches had zero effect on me. None. *Zilch. Nada.*

A couple of days later, I bumped into Mrs. Longo again and told her that I had eaten two peaches but they didn't cool me down.

"Did you eat them cold?" she said smiling. "No, "I said. "I ate them after they had ripened from my fruit bowl."

"Well, they have to be cold" she said with a certain glimmer in her eye. "Try again."

Feeling like a dolt after she left, I thought that maybe eating a COLD peach was the secret, not a peach at room temperature.

I made another trip to the greengrocer and bought more peaches and kept them in the fridge until it heated up again, which was the very next day.

I ate the first cold peach and later in the day, I ate the second one.

Still nothing. I was still hot as hell.

A couple days later I bumped into Mrs. Longo again.

"Did you eat the peaches cold?" she asked.

"Yes, I did," I said. "I was still hot as hell."

"What kind of wine did you use?" she said. "It has to be red wine."

Wine?

Wine? Peaches and wine?

Then it hit me.

Peaches and wine! Cut up peaches in a pitcher of red wine! My grandfather's recipe for the hot weather!

Instantly I was transported to my childhood and visions of my grandfather Alfio Zappalà feeding me a wine soaked, ice cold, slice of the most delicious peach that a seven year old cold possibly taste.

Cold peaches and wine. The Sicilian summer treat that has stood the test of time!

Mrs. Longo had been playing around with me. She knew that if I thought about it long enough, I would remember.

She was right. I remembered.

The next time I saw her I said "Now I understand why you don't get hot, Mrs. Longo. You fooled me, right?"

"No, Alfredo," she said as she threw her head back laughing. "I told you what my father told me a long time ago...eat two peaches a day and you will be fine."

Now that I know how to keep cool on even the hottest of Sicilian day, I always make sure that I have a good supply of peaches and wine on hand.

You can never be too well prepared, right?

That Mrs. Longo...God, I love her.

What a wise woman!

Cinema...Sicilian Style!

Sicily has always been a hot spot for filming movies and no wonder... with its natural beauty, its charm and breath-taking vistas, Italian and American movie stars flock to Sicily to film their movies.

Even though the mafia probably looks over their shoulder as they film, nothing can beat the Sicilian setting for a good movie.

I suspect there will be a lot more movies being produced there in the coming years since Sicily is becoming better and better known.

Hey...maybe I can be an extra to earn a few euro when I'm there!

American actors George Clooney, Brad Pitt and the cast of *Ocean's Eleven* enjoyed themselves while filming there.

So did, Al Pachino, Robert De Niro and Francis Ford Coppola who made their careers while shooting parts of *The Godfather Trilogy* there years ago.

So, why not me?

However, we all have our favorite films about Sicily, and my favorite films were not made with anyone that I just mentioned.

The reason?

Well, I prefer stories and actors that are Italian or Sicilian to really learn the "flavor" of Sicily.

Someone who was born into the culture, so to speak, and also who speaks the language.

Of the hundreds of movies made about Sicily, its people and its customs, I would like to tell you about my three favorite Sicilian movies and recommend that you see them at some point.

They made me laugh, they made me cry and most importantly, they made me understand a bit more about my background.

The first movie I would recommend to you is *Seduced and Abandoned,* a 1964 entrant in the Cannes Film Festival and set in Sciacca.

My friend Jeannie from East Boston originally recommended it to me since her people are from Sciacca, and it was shot in Italian but had a lot of Sicilian dialect too.

The version I saw was sub-titled and easy to enjoy.

The story is a simple yet poignant one: it is the story of a proud Sicilian father trying to save the honor of his daughter and his family after she had been seduced by her sister's fiancée.

I call it a black comedy, but there are many humorous moments in the film.

The very real issues of bride kidnapping known as *fuitina,* a common thing in Sicily up until the 1960s,was used in order to set up a marriage of rehabilitation (called a *matrimonio riparatore*) as a way of salvaging the family's honor.

That is what the father tried to do, and the story is about his attempt to save honor…and face.

Stefania Sandrelli played the part of the "fallen" daughter, and ended up having a very successful movie career. She was a young woman in this movie and her innocent beauty came through loud and clear. What a talented actress.

The scenes of old time Sciacca, the characterization of the gossiping friends of the father, the general angst that the poor man was going through as he tried mightily to save her honor all gave me great thought.

That stuff probably went on every day in real life.

This movie showed me the fundamental differences of growing up as a Sicilian versus as a Sicilian-American.

I highly recommend it, and thank you Jeannie for telling me about it!

On the other hand, *Cinema Paradiso,* shot in 1988 still chokes me up every time I see it, and I have seen it maybe 100 times.

Who can forget the haunting music played throughout this movie? Who can forget the little child Totò and his surrogate father, Alfredo? Who can forget the elegant simplicity of the townspeople and the importance of the local cinema to learn about the outside world?

This movie blew me away the first time I saw it. I literally had a heavy heart after it was over, and I think I actually grieved for Alfredo.

The scene when a grown and successful Totò returned for Alfredo's funeral was a tear jerker. If you don't tear up watching that scene, then you are not human, I think.

Hollywood honored the film by giving it a well deserved Oscar as Best Foreign Film in 1989.

A few years later, a "director's cut" was released that added a few more parts to the story, but I refused to see it, as the movie to me was perfect the way it is.

Like *Seduced and Abandoned* mentioned above, *Cinema Paradiso* is also shot in black and white (well, most of it is, anyway) and sub-titled.

It is probably my favorite movie of all time, actually.

As sad and emotional as *Cinema Paradiso* is, Roberto Benigni's *Johnny Stecchino* is funny.

No...hilarious.

I am sure you know who Benigni is...he won an Oscar a few years back for that poignant World War II movie *It's a Beautiful Life* and maybe I should talk about that wonderful movie too, but *Johnny Stecchino* will give you an excellent idea of Italian humor, the mafia and also has some beautiful shots of Palermo in it too.

Benigni plays the part of a loveable but hapless idiot who just happened to look exactly like a notorious mafia boss named "Johnny Stecchino" who has repented and is in hiding and everyone in Palermo wants to kill him.

"Stecchino" means "toothpick" in Italian...which was what the real bad guy had in his mouth all the time.

There are hilarious scenes in this movie that will make you crazy. One scene when he steals a banana and repents is great. Another scene that is unforgettable is the scene at the opera house (then same opera house, by the way, filmed in *Godfather III*).

Thus, Benigni plays both the idiot and the bad guy to comedic perfection.

The three movies I mentioned merely scratch the surface of great Italian movies.

Need I say Sophia Loren?

However, as a novice Italian speaker, I enjoy watching these sub-titled movies a lot, and learn about my culture at the same time I am learning the language.

Now, please pass the popcorn!

I will talk briefly about the mafia (I do not capitalize the letter "m" in mafia, and neither should you), but really, we Americans have romanced the term far too much.

American movie stars, directors, producers, distributors, record producers and singers have made a living and have laughed all the way to the bank portraying everything Sicilian as "mafia".

I have said it once and I will say it again: Shame on them.

Making a living portraying killers, thugs, drug dealers, and psychopaths is nothing laudable...especially if those characterizations adversely affect your (our) cultural background.

And for those of you who say that these movies are great "art" films, I say this:

Malarkey.

Other than having just a working knowledge of these criminals in general, there is nothing to respect, admire or to emulate when talking about the mafia.

As Sicilians, we all have been painted with the broad brush of "If you are a Sicilian, you must be a mafia person."

This is insulting and demeaning to the 99% of us who are not.

This is insulting to the millions who immigrated to America and honestly made their way through life.

Sicilians are not "one trick ponies"...they are mathematicians, engineers, scientists, doctors, philosophers, artists, poets, nurses, teachers and much more.

Truth be told, the Sicilian mafia has lost its "fast ball" the last couple of decades thanks to the Italian authorities dogged pursuit of them.

Intelligence advances caused in part by the war on terror and advances in money laundering tracking techniques used by law enforcement have resulted in more and more bad guys getting caught and imprisoned.

By "bad guys" I mean the really sophisticated "investment groups" that are really fronts for laundering drug money by the mafia who invest in everything from shopping malls to the local espresso bar.

For example, last summer Italy's anti-mafia fighting force called the DIA seized over twenty million euro from the Calabrian *Ndrangheta* which was operating clandestinely in Rome, disguised as an "investment group" and the seized assets included a busy espresso bar across the street from the prime minister's residence!

Can you imagine that? Romans were shocked as they learned the extent of the penetration of organized crime from Calabria into their city.

For them, this incident struck home.

The Calabrian *Ndrangheta*? Who the heck are they?

Only the biggest, wealthiest, most efficiently run mafia in all of Italy, that's who.

That is because in Italy, there are really four "mafias": the Calabrian *Ndrangheta*, the Sicilian mafia (some people still call it the "Cosa Nostra"), the "Camorra" crime syndicate in Naples, (you have heard of these guys… every time you see mountains of garbage in Naples, these are the guys to blame), and finally the much smaller *Sacra Corona Unita* (United Holy Crown) which operates in the Puglia region.

Collectively, that is the "mafia" in Italy…and is nothing to sneeze at either. While they "talk" to each other and probably coordinate a lot of things, for the most part they are independently operated criminal conglomerates that control a limitless amount of money and power.

However, birds of a feather stick together, so as long as you are not in the drug business, the extortion business, or the business of crime in general, you will never see them or they will never harm you.

As a matter of fact, they will bend over backward to see to it that your holiday vacation in Italy is pleasurable…because they secretly own many hotels and restaurants too!

They are a "shadow" form of entity…influencing everything from business to politicians, to the Catholic Church.

Shocking?

Not really.

The same thing is happening right under your nose in America.

Have you ever thought about all the organized crime groups operating in the United States…from Asia, South America, Jamaica, Mexico,

Russia…plus just "good 'ole boys" from the southern states? Where do you think they launder their money?

Right in the good old USA.

Did you realize that more people have been killed in Mexico's recent drug wars the last few years than brave American soldiers who gave their lives fighting for this county in Vietnam, Korea, The Persian Gulf War, Afghanistan, Iraq and any other post World War II theaters of war?

Not to hurt the feelings of mafia wannabes, but the Sicilian mafia has slipped…and slipped badly…in the world wide power rankings…and I for one am a happy camper.

Maybe…just maybe…as authorities use more and more crime fighting techniques and put more and more bad guys away, then the good people of Sicily…the other 99% of all Sicilians…can have a fighting chance at a life free from this scourge.

As for me, I will continue to speak out against the mafia. As they say in the law: Let them stew in their own juices.

If we use our heads and tax more efficiently some of their illegal activities, then perhaps we can raise revenue at the same time we gut their lifeline…money.

Both here and in Italy.

To those of you that asked: What do I think of the mafia?

Here is the answer:

Not much.

My friend Danielle in Palermo is one piece of work.

He and his uncle own a huge wholesale business that supplies all the tourist shops on the island with all sorts of things like puppets, ceramics, Sicilian flags, Sicilian "Mappinas" (t-towels), decorative carretino and just about every other possible novelty that can be found in any tourist shop from Palermo to Taormina.

I like Danielle because he is one of the few Italian importers that actually buys things from Italian manufacturers that are made in Italy, by real Italians.

Usually, unscrupulous Italian businessmen will buy things from abroad (China, for example), and sell them to unsuspecting tourists as authentic Italian products.

Not Danielle.

Everything he sells is Italian made.

Thus, over the years Massimo and I have done a lot of business with him.

Usually, when I have a big order for him to export to the states, Massimo and I hop in the car and head to Palermo.

Danielle's showroom is huge and the items that he has change from year to year. After we make our selections, we haggle over price, make a deal, then grab a bite to eat with him before heading back to Catania.

Onetime, however, something went a little off track and now that I think about it, I laugh…but believe me, that day that the event happened, neither Massimo nor I were in a laughing mood. Actually, I was, but Massimo certainly wasn't.

I remember the day was scorching hot…it was late July and the searing heat was over ninety- five degrees.

Massimo and I were scheduled to spend the day driving to Palermo to pick up some important samples from Danielle that had just arrived from Milan, and I wanted to take them back to the states with me to show a client.

As we were about to leave (believe me, neither Massimo nor I was looking forward to the drive that day...three hours each way from Catania to Palermo...yuk), the phone rang.

It was Danielle.

"Massimo" he said. "Good news. You don't have to come to Palermo today to pick up Alfred's samples. My cousin has to go to Taormina and I will give them to him. You can meet him there to pick up the items," he said.

Massimo and I were ecstatic. After all, instead of a three hour drive each way, Catania to Taormina took about thirty minutes each way...we were going to save a lot of time.

"Alfred" Massimo said, "Maybe we can go o the beach at La Cucaracha in Catania if we get back early enough."

Since I loved going to the beach on an extremely hot day in order to study the local female population in their native habitat, I nodded my head approvingly.

Off we went to Taormina.

Massimo has the directions in his pocket and I was riding shotgun. We took his car that day...a dark green sports car whose name I have purged from my memory banks.

We zipped on the autostrada and passed all my favorite towns on the way to Taormina.

We zipped past the Aci Reale exit. We zoomed past the Giarre exit, we blitzed past the Fuimefreddo exit. We barreled past the Naxos exit. There it was dead ahead.

The Taormina exit.

One thing though: the traffic was at a standstill at the exit. Half of Sicily decided that day to go to the beach in Taormina.

"Don't worry, Alfred," Massimo said. "I know a shortcut."

Shortcut? Massimo? He gets lost in a circle for heaven's sake, I thought to myself.

Taormina sits atop a mountain after you exit the highway.

To get to Taormina from the exit, it is a cork-screw climb...round and round and round you go...spinning that steering wheel and burning that clutch as you ascend that mountain.

This day was ten times worse: the traffic was bumper to bumper up that steep hill.

185

Attorneys Massimo V. Grimaldi & Alfred M. Zappala. The Dynamic Duo!

Steep hill, you say? Imagine looking up to the sky right now…go ahead, lift your head up high as far as you can…that's where we were headed…in bumper to bumper traffic. Way up there.

Do you know what happens when you are stuck in bumper to bumper traffic as you are going up a nearly vertical mountainwhile driving a stick-shift car? Well, you have to worry about rolling backwards every time you stop, don't you?

This, of course, was the worry of every driver climbing up that mountain that day.

Rolling backwards.

Poor Massimo.

Sweated beaded on his forehead as he fought that clutch. Inch by inch we progressed. Three inches up, one inch backward roll…three inches up…one inch backward roll.

For three hours.

In any case, we made it to the top, and Massimo was drenched with sweat.

Me? I was kinda amused. It was funny, after all, seeing him go absolutely crazy and cursing every one in sight. As mom would say, all the saints in Heaven moved over one inch, he was so mad.

Then, of course, we got lost.

We couldn't find the street that we were supposed to meet Danielle's cousin.

Lido Cucaracha in Catania…a wonderful way to spend a hot day on the beach!

No one, not even the cops, knew where it was.

Finally, Massimo said "Here…I think it is here…I am going to turn right." Which he did.

Except it wasn't a street. It was a passageway. A narrow alley-like passageway about forty-eight inches wide.

Only a dolt would think that was a street.

How narrow was the passageway?

Well, the car got stuck. Wedged right in, wall to wall. He couldn't open his door, and I couldn't open my door.

Squashed.

Ninety-five degrees, in Taormina somewhere, stuck like a sardine in a tin can.

Panic set in with Massimo. "Crap, I am going to dent and scrape the whole car! I was going to trade this in for a new one! Anna will kill me! What should I do?" he cried.

Just as I was about to tell him to put the gear in reverse and the hell with it, we heard a woman's voice.

"Stunatu," she said. "Don't move."

That is not exactly a compliment. It meets "stupid."

This woman just told us "Hey stupid, don't move."

Out of her house came two teenagers and the first thing they did was pull the side mirrors on both sides in.

Then one reached in the car and told Massimo to put the gear in neutral.

Gently, they rocked the car back and forth and it rolled back, freeing itself.

We both had sheepish looks on our face as we then backed out of that narrow pathway.

Finally, after another hour and a half of looking for this non-existent street, we found it.

Come to find out it wasn't a street. It was a private way. A closed passageway where no cars are allowed to travel.

In any case, we parked the car and pounded on the door. No one answered.

Massimo was ready to kill someone, and since I was standing closest to him, I began to worry. He had that glazed, out of his mind look that usually means not guilty by reason on insanity.

Then we heard another voice.

"Are you Massimo?" the voice said.

Massimo replied "Yes! Where is Michele?"

"He got tired of waiting for you guys and went home. The bag you are looking for is under the red car over there."

It was there all right.

Under the red car.

With oil dripping all over it.

From the car.

Drip, drip, drip…right on the garments inside the bag. Ruined.

In any case, the ride home was a little testy.

"I guess this means we are not going to the beach today, huh, Massimo?" I said.

Geez. He didn't even answer.

I think he was mad…or something.

"No, Alfred," he said, "tomorrow we are going to Palermo…and you are going to drive. Now we have to hope that Anna doesn't kill us."

His beautiful wife Anna wouldn't kill me too, would she? I thought.

Hmmm.

Maybe.

Mazara del Vallo......Still Arab
After All These Years

Just below the tip of the westerly point of one of the three "trinicria" points of Sicily...on the southwest side of the island...is a great and historic town named Mazara Del Vallo that I just love to visit.

For centuries, Mazara had been one of the biggest fishing villages in all of Sicily, and her fishermen were legendary seafarers.

While it is still an important fishing community today, the industry (as of all the fishing industry everywhere it seems) is slowing down to a crawl thanks to current economic conditions.

It wasn't always that way, however.

Mazara was founded nearly nine hundred years before the birth of Christ by the ancient seafarers...the Phoenicians.

Its relationship with places like ancient Carthage and North Africa runs deep and true and it epitomizes the true essence of what this world *COULD* be like *IF* the great religions of the world ever decide to live side by side in peace.

I first discovered Mazara years ago when I was looking for a pasta company to build a relationship with in order to import high-grade Sicilian pasta into America.

Finding a Sicilian manufacturer that manufactures pasta according to the FDA guidelines is no easy task...many states require that pasta be "vitamin" enriched, and none of the Sicilian pasta makers put anything extra in their pasta.

Sicilian pasta makers have been making pasta the same way for generations and to hell with what the FDA says, they feel.

"Here is our pasta," a few manufactures told me, "take it or leave it. The FDA is your problem, not ours."

Not wanting to give up the ideas of importing a Sicilian pasta line into America, Massimo managed to find two such companies that manufactured a specific "export" line...vitamin enriched pasta...into America.

Pasta Poiatti was the company we chose, and believe me, Massimo didn't do that much research.

189

Everyone knows Poiatti Pasta in Sicily.

Every market in Sicily sells their brand, and one phone call to the export manager at Poiatti confirmed to us what the rest of Europe was discovering: Sicilian pasta was awesome in taste and texture and yes, they were looking for a US trade partner.

Within a matter of days, we were going west. Massimo and I again were going on one of our legendary road trips!

What makes Sicilian pasta so special? That's easy: The wheat. 100% Sicilian Durum Semolina wheat is used...unaltered by any genetic tampering. The purest of the pure, that's why.

For Massimo, it is always a pleasure for him to accompany me on "American" business trips.

First, it is a pleasant change of pace from the everyday drudgery of practicing law in Catania, and second because he believes (like I do) that he is helping creating Sicilian jobs when we find a product that the American consumer likes.

Arriving in Mazara after a three hour drive, it was obvious that Massimo hadn't a clue where we had to go.

"Let's stop" I said. "We are early for our meeting and I want something to eat."

Somehow, we ended up in the central business district of Mazara, which I later found out was the *Kasbah* district. This had a distinctly Arabic ring to it, I thought to myself.

The buildings in this section also had a distinctly "Arab" flavor to them and we were both now confused.

Walking into a local pizzeria, we struck up a conversation with a man who was a walking encyclopedia on the area.

"Mazara was one of the entry points when the Saracens invaded Sicily," he told us.

"Actually, that happened in nearby Marsala (which means "gate of Allah" in Arabic), but Mazara was quickly occupied by the invaders," he said.

'There wasn't much resistance here because this area had been occupied for centuries by North Africans, especially decedents of the ancient Phoenicians. Even when the Romans occupied it after the fall of Carthage, a lot of the customs stayed. When the Saracens came in at the end of the ninth century, Mazara really blossomed." he proudly said.

Wow. This guy knew his history, I thought to myself.

One look at her waters told us why: Mazara was a natural port and I envisioned hundreds of Saracen ships using this port as a jumping off point for the surrounding areas, and I was correct.

Once the Saracen occupation ended, then fishing became a way of life, supplemented by fertile inland farming areas which produced many different crops.

After eating a delicious lunch and getting our history lesson, we met with the wonderful folks at Pasta Poiatti who fell over themselves being nice to us.

I was shocked to see such a state of the art manufacturing facility in Sicily.

It was really top notch; human hands hardly ever touched the product during the manufacturing process. What's more, everyone who worked there was wearing a white lab jacket and the place was immaculate.

After being duly impressed, we ordered our first (of many) containers of pasta. Our relationship with them lasts until this day.

Several American restaurants in the USA later featured their pasta as their principal pasta and I am happy that many Americans enjoyed their products.

I am most happy, however, to see such a "blended" culture in Sicily…in Mazara.

Today, with the political problems in Egypt and Tunisia, many Tunisians are getting visas and settling in Mazara in exile.

Why not?

They are working the fishing boats, are merchants at the bazaar in the central district, and most importantly feeling like they are among friends with the Sicilians of that region.

Sicily is truly the original melting pot, and every day I seem to realize that a little more.

I truly do.

Youngest kids seem to always get lost in the shuffle.

If you have siblings and are the youngest child, then you know what I mean.

By the time you are old enough to argue with mom and dad, usually they are too tired after having argued with the oldest siblings for so long that they give in a lot.

You probably got to wear a lot of hand-me-downs, too.

Fortunately, I was the eldest in my clan, and always considered myself a "trailblazer" of sorts, but I have had the pleasure to observe for quite a while the youngest of another clan, and have learned much more about life, her giving, her purity of thought and spirit, and more goodness than I thought possible for one person.

Meet Catie Rae Zappalà. My daughter. My little one. She is also a dual US-Italian citizen and she loves her Sicilian identity profoundly.

When she was born, she immediately became the apple in my mom's life. Actually this was true for all my kids and all my brother Tommy's kids... for a period of time...usually until the next sibling or cousin was born, the youngest was the apple of mom's eye...and this continued up until she passed on dating back then on my first grandchild Rosey.

Like my mom was, Catie is a Renaissance woman. It is difficult for me to admit that my daughter is a "woman" as opposed to a "little girl," but she has grown and evolved in life.

As a child, mom sat with Catie and taught her how to "bead," which is essentially making pretty things like Christmas ornaments with beads and pins...a tedious process.

From there, mom exposed Catie to art, drawing, sewing, singing... anything really that pertained to being creative.

Catie and mom, you see, were two peas in a pod. Two fantastically creative people and I was unwittingly observing the knowledge being passed from the eldest to the youngest.

One of the most intensely emotional visuals that I have, as a matter of fact, occurred at mom's wake.

Grandmother and Granddaughter…two Renaissance women.

Hundreds of people showed up that night…my brother Tommy has many friends, my sister Anna, (another of my heroes and a successful executive in the entertainment business) also has many friends and they all showed that evening. My clan and my brother's clan…seven grandchildren in all…were arranged in the reception line pretty much according to age with my brother Tommy standing next to me, and Catie, being the youngest grandchild, at the end of the reception line…way down there.

I remember at one point glancing down the line during that busy evening to check on her and make sure that she was ok.

Briefly our eyes locked.

One glance said it all. I realized how badly she was suffering. I thought to myself that she should be at the head of the line and not me. That glance is forever seared into my memory banks.

Catie is, and will forever be, the free spirit of the family. She is throwback…to another generation…and I admire her for that. Her emotions influence her art, her creativity.

She went on to graduate from art college while studying photography.

While in college, she decided she wanted to learn how to play music. She asked that I buy her an electric guitar. I remember telling her that I would buy her an acoustic guitar instead and when the day came that she played me a song, I would be happy to buy her an electric guitar and amplifier.

Four weeks later, she gave me a private concert. Not only had she learned to play the guitar, she wrote all the songs for her private performance for me! She ended up with that electric guitar…a Gibson Les Paul model…which she now plays with her band "Sway"…a popular Boston band that has recorded three cds over the past five years.

As a photographer, she formed an "artist collective" in Brooklyn, New York where she is living, and her works and those of other fledgling artists and photographers now grace the walls of many different art houses and coffee shops…all for sale, by the way.

Where did she get this talent? It wasn't from me, for sure. I can hardly draw a straight line with a ruler, for heaven's sake. No, it was from my mom. The creative energy of a grandmother was successfully passed on to the grandchild, and the spirits grow together.

I took Catie to Sicily with me. The trip there was a journey of discovery for her and she is hounding me to go back there. I would love it if Catie came to Sicily to get her Master's degree in art or photography and we both could enjoy our ancestral land together.

Someday soon, that will happen. In the meantime, she busied herself with designing the cover of this book, has written more songs, taken more pictures that take your breath away, and generally does things that a Renaissance woman does.

Just like her grandmother.

Spinach Pie From Trecastagni

Today, I will teach you how to make something that will placate your soul. It is an ancient recipe…this one is over a century old…and comes from the hills of Etna.

Many variants exist of this recipe, so feel free to change it, add or delete things once you get the hang of it!

Before I start making this particular specialty of mine for you, I suggest that we both pour ourselves a nice glass of red wine.

Red wine does something to my taste buds and my creativity.

Plus, I have found out that even if the meal that I prepare doesn't turn out well, a half bottle or so of red wine will make me forget that the meal is bad!

In Vino Veritas, no?

However, I know that what I am going to show you today is a terrific meal, and I bet once you get the "knack" down for making this thing, that once a month or so it will be part of your regular food "rotation."

Before you have that glass of wine, you need to run to the market or a bakery for the following ingredients:

From the bakery: two loaves of bread dough. If there isn't a bakery near you, a supermarket will sell frozen bread dough. If you use frozen bread dough, let it defrost first…obviously.

From the market: 2 pounds or 3 pounds (I like a lot) of spinach (either fresh if in season, or in a bag. Honestly, I use "organic" spinach, but "regular" spinach will do.)

You will also need 4 garlic cloves. You should always have garlic cloves on hand. In Italy, it is a deportable offense to be without them.

You will also need some grated Parmesan cheese. Please do not use the cheese in your grocery aisle that is in a paper container. Buy grated IMPORTED Parmesan cheese (from Parma) and the pick up about ¼ pound provolone cheese. Pick up one small can of imported tomato sauce too.

Finally, find some nice black (or brown) pitted Italian olives, and of course, some extra virgin olive oil. You will also need sea salt and black pepper (your salt and pepper shaker will do).

Don't forget to buy a nice bottle of wine too…purely for inspirational purposes…a nice red wine goes well with this meal, although if you must, a nice white wine goes well with this too. To be honest with you, even a nice bottle of beer works well with this meal.

Recap: Ingredients: 2-3 pounds of spinach
2 loaves of bread dough
4 garlic cloves, finely chopped
½ cup to 1 cup grated parmesan cheese
¼ pound provolone cheese, sliced into ¼ inch strips
Black Italian olives, pitted
1 small can of imported tomato sauce
Extra virgin olive oil
Salt and pepper

Utensils:
Cookie sheet
Spatula
Cooking Pot

Now, that you have returned from the market with all the ingredients, pre-heat your oven to 375 degrees. Let it get nice and hot.

NOW you can pour your wine.

The first thing you do is wash the spinach and put it in a pot of water (not much water) for a few minutes. Let it steam until the spinach wilts. Five minutes is plenty of time.

Drain the spinach in a colander and put it aside. Make sure it is well drained!

After ten minutes, place the spinach back in the pot and add in the 4 cloves of garlic which you have chopped, the ½ cup of parmesan cheese, the black olives, about ½ can of that tomato sauce, salt and pepper.

Mix it together…just enough to blend them all…a few times around with a spatula .

Note: the only thing that isn't in that mixture at this point is the provolone strips.

Now, get that cookie sheet and lightly rub olive oil on the sheet…

enough so that nothing will stick.

Get one of the loaves of bread dough, and hand stretch it slowly until it covers the bottom on the cookie sheet. Gently stretch the dough…don't pull it. Pretend you are a pizza maker.

Pour that second glass of wine for yourself, if necessary.

Once the bottom of the sheet is covered with the stretched dough, get the ingredients in the colander and spread them out evenly on the stretched out dough.

Use a fork in necessary, but cover up all the dough with the spinach mixture.

Once that is dozen, drizzle the extra virgin oil on the spinach. Note I said "drizzle"…not "drown."

Now, layer those cut up provolone cheese strips on top of the mixture. Make a nice design if you want!

Almost done!

Finally, get that second loaf of bread dough, stretch it, and gently place in on top of the mixture.

With a fork, "pinch" the edges of the dough all the way around the cookie sheet, closing up the pie.

Pierce the pie several places with the fork too…air holes.

Brush some extra virgin on top of the pie, and bake it in that oven that you have pre-heated for 30 minutes or until the dough turns golden brown.

When done, brush again lightly with extra virgin oil, cover with a cloth and wait ten minutes or so until it "sets."

Cut in slices, and serve.

This is an authentic Sicilian recipe for Spinach pie that comes from Trecastagni originally (my grandmother, Concetta Torrisi) and passed on to my mom. The recipe is over 100 years old…and has stood the test of time!

Enjoy!

By the way, the leftovers keep very nicely in the fridge too!

I bet you will love this one from nanna!

I have to admit it: I am both a political junkie and a die hard sports fan.

Whether it is American politics or Italian politics, American sports or Italian sports, it makes no difference.

I love to read the papers and surf the internet on BOTH sides of the Atlantic Ocean...and follow the goings on of both the political scene and the sports scenes in the USA and Italy.

In America, following politics is far easier than in Italy...by a long shot.

Here we have two parties battling it out every four years. Italy has more parties jockeying for power, and the constant name changes of the parties themselves is very confusing. You practically need a score sheet to keep track of who is who in Italian politics.

Following sports is far easier. The Red Sox, Yankees, Patriots and Celtics have remained unchanged for decades and the rivalries are unparalleled.

Same with Series "A" Soccer in Europe. For example When Catania plays Palermo in a soccer match...Sicily practically closes down! When AC Milan plays Jueventas...same thing.

Despite the fact that we have many political parties in America, either the Democratic Party or the Republican Party has ruled the roost at one time or another for over a century. In America, we have the Green Party, the Socialist Party, the Libertarian Party, the Tea Party...to name just a few...plus a large block of "Independents" which swings one way or the other depending on the state of affairs of the nation at that particular time.

In a broad sense, the majority of Americans are either slightly right of center, slightly left of center, or moderate (center), with both the far right and the far left aggravating everybody.

Thus, whichever party patches a coalition of Independents to their base usually wins a national election as the actual percentage of Democrats and Republicans is very close, making the "swing votes" all the more important.

Italy is the same way. However, being in Sicily when something important is happening in America can be...frustrating. Read on!

I remember when John Kerry was challenging George Bush for the presidency during the height of the Iraq war in 2004.

I was in Sicily at the time and, emotions were red hot.

Blogs and newspapers were ablaze with comments one way or the other about America's involvement and everyone had their two cents to offer as opinion, including myself.

However, the Bush-Kerry debates were headlines...even in Sicily. Since Italy was a US ally in the war in Iraq (a loyal one, by the way), the American election captivated Italy that year.

On the eve of the last Bush-Kerry debate, I was excited to learn that Sicilian television was going to carry the debate. I had been there for a while and was restless for my "political" dose of intrigue and information.

With a six hour time difference between the east coast and Sicily, the 8 PM debate in America translated into a 2 AM debate on Sicilian television.

Big deal.

I was going to stay up and watch that debate, no matter what.

I remember being all fired up for that debate all day.

I couldn't wait. I was psyched for politics.

As the program started, both Bush and Kerry approached their respective podiums and I settled in to watch this epic battle unfold. This was going to be fun, I thought to myself.

Until the moderator asked the first question that is.

The question was asked in English but simultaneously was being translated and dubbed into Italian!

No English except a faint background English was to be heard! Bush's lips were moving in English but Italian was coming out!

The debate was in dubbed Italian...and with my halting knowledge of Italian; I went crazy trying to follow the action!

Neither Bush nor Kerry mentioned the words "pasta," "vino," "pane," "grazie," "dov'è il bagno?" "il conto, per favore," or any of the basic tourist phrases that I knew.

This was going to be a disaster I thought.

In desperation, I remember turning down the sound and trying to read their lips!

George Bush's father once had famously said "Read my lips" in a debate a very long time ago, and here I was, in Sicily...trying to read his son's lips!

Oh brother!

It was awful! What a waste of time!

If that story has you smiling, consider this next one:

Up until the year 2004, the Boston Red Sox had never won a World Series. They had broken my heart many times...especially in 1986 when the Mets beat them that year in the World Series.

In October of 2004, they were playing the hated New York Yankees in a best of seven series for the American League Championship, with the winner going to the World Series.

The Yanks were a powerful team that year, and no one gave the Sox much of a chance. Thus, when I hopped on the plane going to Sicily, and the Yanks beat the Sox in game one, I knew that the better team was probably going to win the series.

In Sicily upon my arrival, the Yanks then won game 2 and also game 3, giving them a 3-0 advantage in the best of seven series.

I was depressed as I checked the scores every day online.

I sighed the same sigh that past generations of Sox fans had done. 'Wait until next year" was a phrase I had heard my whole life.

Then, something strange happened: The Sox won game four...and then game five...and then game six!

Miraculously...they had tied the series 3 games to 3 games and the winner of game seven would go to the World Series!

Boston and Red Sox Nation was going nuts...and so was I ...in Sicily!

There was no way I wasn't going to listen to game seven! No way I was going to read lips this time!

They had a chance to beat the Yankees, after all, and head to the World Series.

In any case, I searched high and low in Sicily for somewhere to watch the game. No luck.

That six hour delay made for a 2 AM start in Sicily, and no one was going to stay up and watch American baseball.

To make matters worse, my crummy computer had no speakers, so I could not even listen to the game on Armed Services Radio.

Thus, I had to READ the game.

Yes, that is right. I went online and READ the game as it happened.

Pitch by pitch, play by play.

With no crowd roaring, no visual effects, just sentence after sentence on a computer screen. No peanuts, no popcorn, no bottle of beer, nothing.

From 2 AM until 5 AM, I remember going out of my mind reading that damn screen.

My neighbors must have thought I was nuts, because when someone homered, I yelled out loud! I was a nervous wreck and couldn't contain my excitement.

Finally the last ...and most important...sentence appeared on my screen: "Grounder for the last out...Red Sox win. They go now to World Series."

That is how I found out that the Sox beat the Yanks. On a computer screen, in Sicily, in the dead of night, by myself... yelling at the top of my lungs... sitting in front of my computer screen in my boxer shorts.

(Sigh)

I suppose I should tell you that this was the manner that I "watched" the Sox win the World Series that year. Yup. That happened online too.

Want to know a bigger secret? This was the same way that I learned they won *ANOTHER* World Series four years later. Again online.

Want to know yet another secret?

This was the exact same way I learned that my beloved Patriots won TWO Super Bowls too. Online and while in Sicily. I have never been in country when either the Sox or the Patriots won their respective championships!

Now, here is the ultimate irony: Guess where I was when Italy beat France to win the World Cup? Correct. In the USA.

(Sigh). Oh well...at least they won!

If you think American politics is a rough and tumble game, you should investigate Italian politics.

Investigate?

Why not? Just about every Italian politician gets "investigated" at one time or another. Investigating politicians in Italy is a national sport. Everyone gets investigated at one time or another it seems.

I think a better choice of words might be "familiarize yourself"…or do what most Italians do…they "isolate themselves" or "just don't trust" them.

I once counted how many Italian governments have rises and fallen since the end of the Second World War. Over sixty.

That's right…there have been over sixty governments formed since 1946. *Pazzo*. (That means "crazy" in Italian.) Very *pazzo*.

Did you know that Sicily is an autonomous region of Italy and was granted autonomy on May 15, 1946, eighteen days **BEFORE** the newly formed Italian government came into existence, which was on June 2, 1946?

Now you see the problem with Sicilians who want autonomy…they have always believed that 'Italy' never stuck to its side of the bargain post World War II and gave them lip service with an "autonomy agreement" just to get them in the national fold.

Did you know that Sicily actually has a "president"….who is a member of the European Parliament, heads the minority national party "Movement For Autonomy"…and was born in Catania? His name is Raffaele Lombardo.

If you are going to check out Raffaele Lombardo on an internet search, you mind as well check out Salvatore "Totò" Cuffaro… the former president of Sicily who was convicted in 2008 of passing state information to the mafia.

(Sigh)

The French say it perfectly: "Plus ca change, plus c'est la meme chose"……The more things change, the more they stay the same.

(Sigh)

In any case, the beat rolls on with daily Italian politics, and I am a fascinated observer.

Here are the basics (actually, there are many similarities between the American form of governance and the Italian form), but this will give you a general flavor and maybe whet your appetite for further study on your part.

Before I start however, you should know that the Italian legal system is a lot different than ours.

In America, our rule of law is based on the 'English Common Law", while Italian law is based on the Napoleonic Code, Roman law, and statutes. It is a blended form of law with different principles.

In Italy, when someone "renounces" someone with the police, it is a big deal.

In any case, Italy has a president who serves a largely ceremonial role...almost like a king.

He attends events, cuts ribbons, and when the government falls, he is the one who is supposed to stir the pot again, pull out a few more rabbits and appoint an interim government until elections can be held. He also acts as the Commander In Chief of the armed forces.

The current president is Giorgio Napolitano.

By the way, the Italian Armed Forces are excellent. They have been a loyal US ally in the War on Terror and their intelligence services on terrorism are considered to be one of Europe's best.

The real power in the Executive Branch of government is held in the Chamber of Deputies...roughly akin to an American president's Cabinet, and the Chamber of Deputies is headed by the Prime Minister.

The Prime Minister calls the shots in Italy.

Since 1994, Silvio Berlusconi has been the Prime Minister. He is one of the wealthiest men in Europe and controlled the nation's media (television and print) before entering politics.

However, he was always a "behind the scene" power broker.

There has been a strong "link" ...(I like that word...this is a delicate way of accomplishing what I am trying to say)...between him and other "power brokers" in Sicily, and Sicily has consistently backed him in elections.

Lately, however, due to a series of dumb moves allegedly made with a young woman, he has been all over the world's newspapers being charged with this or that and being prosecuted for this or that.

His popularity, as a result, has taken a serious hit. It makes no difference.

Say what you want about the guy (honestly, despite his flaws, I like him), he has been a champion against the War on Terror despite intense opposition to the war in Italy.

He announced recently that he will not seek re-election in 2013 and has endorsed a Sicilian, Angelino Alfano, to succeed him. It doesn't seem that Alfano is the most popular guy on the planet right now though.

Alfano was the author of an unpopular law called the "Lodo Alfano" which gave immunity to the President, both Presidents of the Legislative branch, and the Prime Minister.

The law was later declared unconstitutional, and his popularity suffered as a result. Plus people seem to feel that he will be in Berlusconi's back pocket if elected.

However, he has had a meteoric career in politics, having been a big shot in Berlusconi's "Forza Italia" party and its successor party "People of Freedom" (PDC), and is a member of the Chamber of Deputies representing Sicily since 2005.

The Chamber of Deputies, which is a bicameral Chamber (like our Congress), has 630 members. The Senate has 315 members...plus people who are appointed "senators for life"

That means that in the Legislative branch of Italian government... there are 915 men and woman...from many different backgrounds and philosophies...trying to make laws and run things there!

In America we have 100 senators and 435 members of the House of Representatives, making for 535 people messing things up...in a country of over 300 million.

Italy has nearly double the amount of politicians...in a country of only 60 million!

Now you understand why things move so slow in Italy!

Try to get 915 Italians to agree on anything...that will never happen!

No matter what party is in power, however, the goings is always rough and tumble.

This is why I love it so!

Smokey is what I call it.

If I were a painter, the term would be called "*sfumato.*"

Pronounced (sfoooomaaaatow)

In New England, the word we would is the word "veiled" or "vanishing" or "smokey" or "hazy".

I like *sfumato* more.

I heard it used once in Rome by someone who was describing the art technique of the da Vinci School of the Renaissance painters. Those who painted an object as if it was veiled slightly, or like a photograph shot in low light were know as *sfumato* painters.

Take the Mona Lisa, for instance. The technique was developed by Leonardo da Vinci and many Renaissance painters followed suit. Today, the Russian Impressionist use it a lot.

Look at the Mona Lisa: you will understand.

That is how the sun rises in Sicily: *sfumato* style. It rises in this veiled and smokey manner, bursting a few moments into a brilliant clarity.

That fifteen minute window of the rising sun in the morning is my favorite time of the day.

My *sfumato* time.

The barely glistening Sicilian sun has only a faint glimmer as it rises. As it awakes from a night's slumber, it gently comes to life. Then in a flash it goes away.

The eyes are the first to enjoy the sight.

The air at that time of the early day is *sfumato* as well. I just coined that description of the air. Really it is a combination of the air, the texture of the light and the smell of the morning sea that together in unity creates the image that burns into my brain every day.

There is no other place on earth that has this combination, I think. Sunrise in Sicily is a wonder of nature, and later in the day, sunset in Sicily is too.

The Sicilian sunrise puts almost all the senses together: the eyes, the nose, the ears.

Since I never speak during this period, only the mouth isn't used. Three out of four senses does the job just fine for me.

Then suddenly, it goes away. The *sfumato* vanishes into daylight.

As the sun rises, the haze clears and vision is restored with a brilliant clarity.

It stays that way all day…until the sun decides to sleep for the night. For you see, the Sicilian sunset rivals the sunrise. *Sfumato* returns briefly at sunset too.

I have witnessed the rising and setting sun in Sicily from many locations and many angles.

From the sea side to the valleys. From the mountain top to the plains. It is always the same: An endless video loop of profound beauty that has played repeatedly since the beginning of time.

I wonder how you will feel the first time you experience this.

The Sicilian morning sun is compelling; like many hundreds of generations of Sicilians, it calls them out for a new day. Sicilians live for the day. Sicily's history has taught them this.

I need an espresso to fully complete the effect. I need to tie all my senses together. My mouth needs to get involved somehow in the senitory unity taking place, and if I do not talk, I can at least taste.

An espresso sipped in solitude…while the Sicilian sun rises…ties it all together.

During the evening, a glass of red wine is the able substitute.

As I raise my glass later in the day to silently toast the setting Sicilian sun, I think of my friends in Rome…especially my friend Luigi Frare… the elegant and now retired barman at the exquisite hotel at the top of the Spanish steps, The Hassler Hotel.

"Alfred" he once said to me. "Do you know where the phrase "chin-chin" comes from as Italians toast each other?"

Since I did not, here is what he told me:

"When you pour a glass of wine and hold it to the light, the eyes appreciate its beautiful color. Nature has created a thing of beauty and your eyes enjoy the result" he said.

"When you gently twirl the wine around the glass and smell its wondrous bouquet, your nose and sense of smell also enjoy the sensation" he said.

"When you taste the delicious wine, even your mouth and its taste buds are involved and are happy" he said.

"But do you know what senses isn't happy, Alfred?" he asked.

"Your ears. They cannot enjoy the wine."

"So we say "chin-chin" as we toast so that all the senses are involved when we celebrate the vino."

Smart man, that Luigi.

Thus, every night, as the Sicilian sunset sets, I hold up my glass of wine and I too say "Chin-Chin".

I always say 'Grazie a Dio" too.

I thank the original artist who created this scene, the Good Lord, and ask Him every night to protect her and her people.

I toast the Sicilian sunset...*sfumato* scene and all! Know what the best part is?

Tomorrow morning, when I get up from my evening slumber, the sunrise will be waiting for me again...for a very brief moment!

And then it starts again.

The Sicilian Project

We need to communicate better with our Sicilian brethren if we ever hope, as Sicilian-Americans, to lift Sicily from the bottom of the heap and take her to her rightful place at the top of the heap.

If we all pitch in and help, we can do it.

Let's use our AMERICAN noodles here and get creative.

There are, after all, *TWICE* as many descendants from Sicily here in America as there are Sicilians in Sicily!

In the states, there are nearly twelve million Sicilian-Americans, making them the largest of all the Italo-American groups.

In Sicily, there are not even six million Sicilians.

Thus, our population of Americans with Sicilian blood DOUBLES what remains in Sicily.... not to mention the hundreds of thousands more who live in Australia, South America and the rest of the world.

It is time for us here in America to *organize ourselves* and attempt to do the impossible: actually do something positive for our cultural brothers and sisters...our *paesani*.

I am calling this initiative "The Sicilian Project" and will begin working on it immediately.

Maybe you want to help. Read on!

However, this has to be done in a stealth manner, as for the most part, two obstacles have to be circumvented, obstacles that if permitted to get involved in any way, would end up just lining their pockets instead of accomplishing the objective.

I am talking about doing something positive for Sicily despite a largely indifferent government and the mafia.

Can it be done? Yes definitely.

If we use our heads a bit.

To me, education has always been the key.

If you teach someone how to plant wheat, then they will learn to feed themselves.

Sicilians are very intelligent people. They are highly intelligent, actually... capable of greatness in the world, if given the opportunity.

Truth be told, many already have achieved greatness in the world… in many areas.

To me, the greatest thing that we could give a youngster, a high school student, a college student, a recent graduate, or a young business person in Sicily is the ability to speak and read and understand the English language.

A fluent Sicily would be able to bootstrap itself out of its economic doldrums and slingshot itself into prominence. It already has its most important asset in place: the Island itself, its location, and its natural wonders.

These assets must be now honestly and intellectually utilized in a manner that will not strip her of these resources, but rather in a manner that will assure that they last in perpetuity.

What about the mafia? Since what I am talking about is not a criminal enterprise, they will barely lift their head as they count their money.

The mafia has no interest in helping bootstrap the young. Thus, by educating them, sooner or later the weak shall become the strong.

History has proved this countless times over the millennia.

My view is simple: learning centers should be created…maybe one

Luigi Frare, the now-retired barman at the Hassler Hotel in Rome. He taught me much about Roman traditions. No visit to Rome is complete without a drink in this wonderful bar located at the top of the Spanish steps.

or two at first...but expanding as the years pass...controlled by American-Sicilians and located in key urban and then rural areas in Sicily...that teach Sicilians the basics of the English language and ways to improve themselves in life.

American-Sicilians could be sent there to live, absorb the culture, learn about their ancestral roots themselves...and in return teach Sicilian students the English language.

A cross-pollenization of cultures, so to speak.

One helping the other.

I envision a non-profit organization similar to a mini-version of the Peace Corps being formed...open to all Americans...from the young to the retired.

With one mission: teach English to Sicilian people.

Impossible, you say?

Let us examine the extraordinary power and influence that America Jews have over their ancestral country of Israel as a learning tool please. Let's use them as our example.

Wealthy Jewish-American philanthropists have set up many organizations that send college age students to Israel in order to inter-react with their brethren there. Every year, hundreds of high school and college kids spend the summer teaching, working, helping, and learning.

Since the founding of Israel, as a matter of fact, American Jewry has been the central source of money, education, knowledge and power for the fledgling country.

Not only has actual good work been done "on the ground" by these people in Israel, but today the American-Jewish lobby is perhaps the single biggest influence on Israeli politics.

Why can't we attempt a smaller version of that...for Sicily?

Sadly, most "Italian-American" organizations haven't come near the level of success that their American-Jewish counterparts have.

Why?

There are many reasons. A disinterested Italian government has been the major impediment in my view...but I think that can be changed.

Civic organizations like the Sons of Italy are wonderful, but what I am talking about is a targeted organization with a single mission: teaching

210

English to students AND to teachers there. Let's teach the teachers HOW to teach English.

Sicilians helping Sicilians…like it always has been.

In my mind's eye, I would like to see a group of Americans "adopt" a town or city and begin a cultural exchange program with a "boots on the ground" mentality.

In other words, things being controlled for the most part here, from America.

Perhaps this can be started in one area. Or two areas. And, as time passes and word spreads, it can be expanded.

Perhaps some sort of exchange program can be formed and universities, colleges, and other professional schools could be involved.

Maybe I am a dreamer, but I bet that one of you reading this book will get that glimmer of genius in his or her eye and come up with an even better idea…and want to get involved in some manner.

What the heck. Contact me…I will be in Sicily in any case.

I will be helping my people there in any case.

We will call it "*The Sicilian Project.*"

After all, that is why I am returning to my homeland.

I will be the first "boot on the ground" and will engage any and every person I know to help on this project. I will be happy when I see progress there in this one area.

I know that many of you dream of one day going to Sicily and experiencing first hand the wonders of the Island. However, active involvement is something of this nature would make your visit profoundly more satisfying and fulfilling.

Why not?

Let's do something constructive and pitch in!

Yesterday I dragged my grandfather's trunk upstairs from the basement and placed it in the middle of my living room.

It's time to begin to get Gaetano's Trunk ready for its return trip home.

It's time to pack the trunk. It's been a long time. It has patiently waited for this day for one hundred and three years.

This past year, I have been very busy making preparations for the move to Sicily. Uprooting myself and moving out of country is no easy task, I have discovered. There are still a million things to do, it seems.

Fortunately, the "big stuff" is done in Sicily. I have a beautiful place to live and it is all furnished and waiting for me; I have a newly purchased (used) car in good condition to get me around when I arrive.

I have a nice couple who rent the upstairs rooms and help me pay the expenses.

Most importantly, I have my permanent resident card.

I am officially a resident of Aci Catena, Sicily.

A lot of work still needs to be done though. I need to settle in and get a daily "work" routine established. I need to support myself. The bad American economy has wiped out my savings. However, my biggest asset remains: my ability to survive. I am a survivor…ingrained in me since birth. I am unafraid of the future. I will make it somehow, as I always have.

In any case, today I brought the trunk up from the basement, and it sensed that I was coming. I single-handedly carried the thing up the stairs myself. It helped me, I swear.

When I opened the trunk, just like a scene out of a movie, I felt sunlight burst out of it. Not really, but that is what I expected. How did I feel?

Elated. That's the word. And excited too.

The inside of the trunk is in surprisingly good shape considering it was shipped here one hundred and three years ago. No mold, no smell… practically new.

Two of the locks are broken, but it makes no difference: I am going to place a sturdy strap around the trunk to secure it after I pack it, then shrink wrap it.

Taormina has many interesting places tucked away on side streets and passageways. It is always an adventure walking around this beautiful town.

Finally I will put it on a pallet and have it shipped to Sicily.

In 1908 my grandfather arrived in America with twelve dollars in his pocket. In today's dollars, that would be exactly $293.00.

I decided that is exactly how much money I will have in my wallet the day I fly back too. While I hope to have substantially more to fall back on upon my arrival, somehow that amount is an appropriate amount.

Big differences exist between his arrival in the states and my arrival in Sicily though. He was 18 years old when he arrived. I am 61 years old when I depart. He had his whole life ahead of him. I am doing the final lap of life, I think. Maybe not though.

Funny, I feel 18 years old.

More differences than age exists, though: he was trained as a blacksmith and a winemaker in Sicily. I was trained as an educator, writer and lawyer in America.

Some things are similar though: he arrived here during a bad economic time in Sicily. I am arriving in Sicily in a bad economic time.

It makes no matter.

He was a survivor. So am I.

As I look around, the first thing I have to decide is what to take, what to give away, what to sell, what to donate.

All I plan to take with me is my clothes…and prized possessions that will be carried within this trunk.

I have an old photo of Gaetano and his wife Concetta. I have another old photo of my grandfather Alfio Zappalà his wife Agostina. They haven't been back to Sicily in a century.

Today, they will start the process of returning home. I place their photos in the trunk.

I also place photos of my great grandfather Mateo Zappala too that I found and also that of my great grandmother Maria Zappala. Their photos go in the trunk.

So does the picture of my uncle Frank Lascola…my favorite great uncle and also born in Sicily. Frank did return to Sicily once though. In 1944, he returned to Sicily is a US army uniform and helped Patton chase the Germans out of Sicily.

He deserves to go. I place his picture in the trunk.

So does a picture of my uncle Jimmy Polozzotti. He deserves to go. He married my grandmother's sister Mariaeta and sponsored many Italian immigrants to come to America and find a new life. He was a humble elevator operator, but he deserves to go. This is his first trip there. He would be 102 years old today.

I figure that I will take a picture of my father and mother too…not that I need one…as their images are burned into my brain, but it was a promise that I made to my father on his deathbed that compelled me to go to Sicily in the first place, starting this "magnificent obsession" that I have.

I place a few more photos in there too; sentimental ones of relatives long since passed but holding *Sicilia Bedda* dear to their hearts.

Actually, I find myself getting a little emotional as I stare at faded images. It strikes me that this trunk is as much theirs as mine now.

As my package of photos get larger and larger, I realize that I am not alone on this return trip. It looks like I will have a lot of company. It looks like I will be able to make a lot of spirits truly rest in peace.

I am happy.

This is the least I can do. Almost all of them sacrificed their lives for their family...willingly, silently, gladly.

Time to pay them back. It needs to be paid back. I need to re-pay the debt.

I honestly haven't a clue what to expect in Sicily when I finally give up my condo and have no "home" in America.

I will be a "Stranger in a Strange Land," just like that character Micheal Valentine Smith in Robert Heinlein's famous book of a space visitor coming to earth. Gosh, that book was always one of my favorites, and now I am going to live it for real. I am a stranger.

I must be crazy.

I have a few things going for me, however: I have my wits, my intelligence, my profession.

Somehow I will manage to survive...and I not only intend to survive, I intend to prosper

I need to show people that what I am doing is for the love of country and for the love of people whose blood course my veins and that of my ancestors blood of two millennia.

I will observe, I will write, I will experience things with my friends. I will continue to paint pictures with words for you.

Thank God that I have my "partner in crime" Massimo. Who the heck knows what kind of adventures we will find in the next year. We will laugh and go crazy, but we will have fun.

Thus, I am far better equipped to "reverse immigrate" than my grandfather. I already have a home, friends, a profession, and despite the fact that I am taking a symbolic $293 with me, I have the capacity to earn more and support myself.

I will return to America frequently. I will continue to teach at my beloved law schools for compacted periods of time.

I will spend probably more time with the children and grandchildren than I do now.

I know they will end up spending time with me in Sicily too.

A family remembered: grandparents Torrisi, my parents, grandparents Zappalà.
They made me who I am today.

No, my job is not done…not by a long shot. I am not fading into oblivion. Rather, I am turning the page on an already magical life and starting yet another adventure.

Next year at this time, I hope to have another book out.

I will try to continue to show you through my whimsical writings something that we both love.

I will blog on my website, practice law for those Americans who need help in Sicily ot Italy, and speak about my *Sicilia Bedda*.

Nope, I am not finished.

I am just starting, actually.